The Dissolution of the Medieval Outlook

The Dissolution of the Medieval Outlook

An Essay on Intellectual and Spiritual
Change in the Fourteenth Century

Gordon Leff

New York • NEW YORK UNIVERSITY PRESS • 1976

To Eric James

Contents

Preface

The purpose of this book is expressed in its title. It is an essay, an attempt to explore the ways in which the medieval outlook on the world was changing and giving place in the fourteenth century to new consessions that were ultimately to bring its supersession. It is not a survey, still less a textbook, but rather a delineation of what seem to me to have been the areas of fundamental change. It is, therefore, one individual's interpretation, much though it owes to others.

I. Orientations

Every so often accepted ways of thinking are called into question and there is a reassessment. It need not be total or sudden or unanimous—it rarely if ever is—and it can occur at any level, from the individual to the cosmic. But to be intellectually significant it must meet two conditions: of being of a public as opposed to a private nature and of modifying the prevailing modes of thought. Like any change it will be more or less significant according to how far it goes.

Now the problem is to assess that significance. Unlike changes in natural phenomena that can, in principle at least, be measured exactly, there is no exact means of measuring intellectual change which is not itself about what can be measured or known exactly. And since exact knowledge in the modern sense only properly begins in the seventeenth century, the greater part of previous thought, as well as much subsequently—including most philosophy and theology—falls outside its ambit. However completely a system of thought may be known, it can still be understood divergently, indeed contradictorily, as the diverse, often conflicting, schools of thought, as old as thought itself, to say nothing of the different schools of interpreting them, testify. Even those past ideas of nature that are open to scientific evaluation are more appropriately judged not for their correctness or incorrectness—a test few would survive—but for their fruitfulness in the light of subsequent knowledge. Moreover, in the context of intellectual change, there is the further limitation imposed by the criterion of influence: many potentially fertile ideas in advance of their time, from John of Philipon's in the sixth century to Leonardo da Vinci's in the sixteenth, have been passed over for ideas less advanced, which have nevertheless been the path to greater advance. Consequently the criteria of intellectual change can in the end only be contextual: in terms of how and with what effects an outlook or a system differed before and after certain developments, independently of or despite the intrinsic worth ascribed to it.

The changes with which this book is concerned are principally philosophical and theological and at a time—the earlier and middle decades of the fourteenth century—when such change was almost wholly conceptual rather than from new empirical discoveries. It thus consisted essentially in the reinterpretation of received ideas and the formulation of new ones on the basis of new meanings rather than new knowledge.

Accordingly, I shall begin by attempting to define what I understand by an outlook and significant change in relation to it, first in general and then in the context of the fourteenth century; and state the reasons for regarding the changes in the fourteenth century as the beginning of the end of the medieval outlook. The following three parts will consider those changes in their specific aspects.

What we call an outlook is an abstraction or more strictly a set of abstractions formed from our idea of the ideas, attitudes, and beliefs of different individuals or groups. It does not therefore stand for anything in particular, but is a mental construct composed of diverse concepts that becomes more abstract the more composite it is. For the further removed our concepts are from the nonconceptual the more they owe their meaning to the categories we impose upon them. It is there that the divergencies over them arise. An ascending order of abstraction is accompanied by an increasing arbitrariness of generalization. Where physical concepts can be in principle reduced to the things they denote, even if those things cannot always be directly encountered, concepts composed of other concepts, and which are not directly of real things, are reducible only to further concepts. Thus the concept of man as a physical species is convertible with real individual men of whom it can be verified empirically; beyond differences in the conventional terms standing for man it will mean the same for everyone. Man, however, conceived as a rational being or a social animal or creature made in God's image, will not, because there is no such direct correspondence. Each of these expressions is a collection of concepts—of rationality, sociality, divinity, creation, and so forth—which separately or in combination has no natural nonconceptual counterpart as something actually existing or separately identifiable. Regardless of where their truth is held to lie—as merely generalizations from human behavior or as real expressions of human nature—their status remains purely conceptual. In contrast to actual knowledge of real things, which is independently corroborable of our concepts, conceptual knowledge is inseparable from them: however many men we may encounter whom we define as reasonable or sociable or God's creatures, we can do so only by means of those very concepts used to define them. The only men who continue to exist are individual men.

That does not mean that conceptual knowledge is necessarily of what is nonexistent or whatever we choose to conceive as real. But rather that it owes its identity to our conceptions. The problem is precisely to correlate them with what we take to be reality in default of any verifiable correlation between conception and reality. Not only has that resulted epistemologically in an irreducible diversity of interpretations of the same phenomena, from the nature of knowledge itself to the nature of the world, which, so far at least, can only be partially resolved by science. Methodologically, in relation to an outlook—our concern here—it has two consequences. The first is that the unity we ascribe to, or imply in, an outlook by the use of such expressions as the Enlightenment or Christian philosophy is a fictitious one. They are labels for a series of disparate ideas and activities by disparate individuals at disparate times and places. Only through combining them at the furthest degree of abstraction beyond specific modes or thinkers can their differences be overcome; that is, by subsuming them under some generic term defined by reference to another such term, as an outlook is called Christian or enlightened by contrasting it with outlooks which are neither. That applies equally to the subgroups, of systems, schools, and doctrines, composing them. The characteristics with which we endow them are not of self-subsisting species of thought but arrangements of ideas according to their affinities. In making intellectual ones the organizing principle we exclude, or at least subordinate, other affinities—of nation, milieu, loyalty, temperament—which may for those concerned have been primary.

An outlook then at any level is formed from a perspective that cannot be or have been that of the agents themselves to whom it is attributed; where it is of the past it also stands outside time, giving ideas or individuals a configuration in the light of subsequent events and changing with them: St. Thomas Aquinas or Thomism does not have the same import in 1270 as in 1570 or 1870 because of what has supervened. Like a mountain seen from different positions there is no exclusive viewpoint. But where a mountain remains for human purposes constant, an outlook can shift with a single thinker and is at the least modified from generation to generation until it becomes something different. To define it is always to petrify it, making of it a still that is taken from only one aspect. Like any such classification it says at once too little and too much.

That brings us to the second consequence. An outlook is not uniformly diffused and does not follow a single direction. It is like a series of Chinese boxes, which have in common their existence at a certain time. Even if we can find an epitome in a particular individual or system or phase, as Leonardo da Vinci is frequently made to personify the Renaissance ideal, or Thomism medieval scholasticism, it is usually only one box; some like Savonarola do not fit at all. Nor are the ideals which are held in common, like Christianity in the Middle Ages, universally understood in the same way. There is not just one wavelength connecting all members of a society. They belong to different conceptual worlds according to their place in the real one, as members of a particular group, and the concepts they bring to it. These are not necessarily identical or invariable to all who share it. A peasant's understanding of the world is unlikely to be a theologian's, or a theologian's a physicist's. But neither need each be that of all peasants or theologians or physicists. There have always, at least from the time of the Greeks, been conceptual worlds within worlds, expressed in the diverse traditions, schools and systems which have coexisted in almost every epoch. It is therefore misconceived to suppose an unbreakable unity between every branch of knowledge or that intellectual development depends upon a common set of beliefs. Far from rising or falling in unison, they evolve unevenly. The Middle Ages had one faith but divergent philosophical—and indeed theological—systems; the modern world has one science while knowledge and belief are fragmented.

Hence there is not—or only exceptionally—a single view of reality governing all understanding. What we identify as an outlook is rather a certain framework of commonly held absolute presuppositions about the meaning of reality—as they concern God, man, nature, society, the universe— mediated in varying degrees of coherence and articulateness by the conceptual worlds coming within it. Which in a formative sense means those of the theologians and the physicists and the other intellectual agents rather than of the peasants and those who are the recipients. The ways in which that happens give an outlook its shape, taken at any one time or over a period. It can be said to continue so long as the same presuppositions hold. When they no longer do so continuity ends. Change then becomes discontinuous and, in terms of an outlook, fundamental. For regardless of the form it takes it marks the displacement of an existing framework, whether gradually, as in the transition to a modern from a medieval outlook which was for long incomplete, or through the disintegration of any common framework, as in the twentieth century, which cannot properly be said to have common presuppositions—as opposed to expectations—at all.

Such a development has its beginnings in a shift back in the order of discourse from what can be said in the light of certain accepted first principles to those principles considered for themselves. Or in modern jargon from the data to the hypotheses or paradigms explaining them. That does not entail their rejection; it can as well be to reaffirm them: initially it usually is. The difference is that from having been the basis of inquiry they enter into discussion as the subject of inquiry. And that is when they for some reason appear as a no longer adequate means of explanation or as inferior to others. In a general sense that is of course true of all conceptual change. It arises from a discrepancy between explanation and what is to be explained, whether expressed empirically in the failure to account for the facts as they are taken to be, or formally and speculatively in the anomalies between theoretical conceptions related as premises and conclusions, the characteristic medieval form. In each case that leads either to readjustment or to competing interpretations. To that extent it applies to any change, whether it falls within or outside the prevailing modes.

Here, however, the operative distinction is between continuous and discontinuous change. Both may be far reaching; neither need be from conscious design as so many fundamental developments have been one and not the other. But whereas continuous change is through divergent interpretations within an existing conceptual framework and so in some kind of

conjunction, discontinuous change is the result of divergent reinterpreta-
tions of that framework leading finally to a disjunction in divergent frame-
works. For that it does not have to be global but can begin, as most
scientific change has usually begun, from the need to restate problems
having no apparent immediate implications for an outlook as a whole.[1]
While such modifications may in detail provide a new coherence, the total
effect is of growing incoherence in the loss of an overall definition through
revision or questioning of hitherto accepted notions. Paradoxically that
incoherence is accentuated by the very effort to save the concepts in need
of clarification, for it introduces a series of competing redefinitions rather
than a general reformulation embracing them. That can come only with
the cumulative rethinking that makes a comprehensive alternative feasible
and acceptable.

The complete process from one such framework to another only properly
occurs in the different branches of science which beyond particular hypotheses depend for their coherence upon certain universally acceptable hypotheses, even if they are competing. Elsewhere, in philosophy and theology,
the one common conceptual framework, of a Christian philosophy, ended
with the Middle Ages; it has been replaced not by another comparable
outlook but by self-contained philosophies and theologies together with the
separate sciences into which knowledge has since been divided and upon
which philosophy and theology, to an extent, themselves draw. Correspondingly philosophical and theological change, and with them conceptual
continuity and discontinuity, have lost their universal import in an intellectual constellation where there is no fixed center.

That brings us to the fourteenth century; for it seems to me that it was
then that this differentiation effectively began. It thereby inaugurated the
displacement of the medieval world view and exemplifies the discontinuity
which we have been considering.

Two principal elements were involved. On the one hand a rethinking of
the bases of philosophical and theological truth; and on the other an
attempt to explain the natural world in natural terms. The first involved

1. For scientific change see T. S. Kuhn, *The Structure of Scientific Revolutions*, 2d ed.
(Chicago, 1970), who, however, overstates the disjunctive element at the expense of the
cumulative effect of scientific development.

establishing the conditions of natural certainty and the different criteria regulating knowledge and belief; the second the investigation of natural phenomena in physical, mathematical, and logical, as opposed to metaphysical, terms, according to the object of inquiry. Together they changed the existing modes of discourse not through rejecting the framework of Christian, Aristotelian, and Neoplatonic suppositions in which they had been conducted, but in bending it to new interpretations. In that sense one outlook was not substituted for another. The change was over how the same one should be understood. It was accompanied by a rethinking of the spiritual criterion regulating religious life and gave a new focus to Christian thought.

In general terms it was diverted from the predominantly speculative channels, in which it had hitherto run almost unbrokenly from the time of St. Augustine, to a systematic exploration of the scope and limits of knowledge. The effect was largely to transform the notion of what could be known and its relation to what must be believed. Over the preceding two centuries in particular the area of speculation had been extended to embrace whatever was conceivable by faith, reason, or experience. Although the demarcation between them became in the thirteenth century increasingly sophisticated—in some cases sophistical—and contentious, and led to the condemnation in 1277 by the ecclesiastical authorities at Paris of 219 propositions drawn from the discussions in the arts faculty of the university for expressing a predominantly naturalistic standpoint inimical to Christian faith,[2] the assumption persisted for another two genera-

---

2. For these events and the disputes leading to them, the following may be consulted: E. Gilson, *History of Christian Philosophy* (London, 1955) and G. Leff, *Paris and Oxford Universities in the Thirteenth and Fourteenth Centuries* (New York, 1968). Subsequent discussion will assume familiarity or consultation with these or other works, not subsequently cited, of which a few may be suggested. No attempt has been made here or throughout to be comprehensive: C. Bérubé, *La Connaissance de l'individual au Moyen Age* (Paris, 1964); F. C. Copleston, *A History of Medieval Philosophy* (London, 1972, New York, 1975); A. C. Crombie, *Robert Grosseteste and the Origins of Experimental Science, 1100–1700* (Oxford, 1953); A. Forest, F. Van Steenberghen, M. de Gandillac, *Le Mouvement Doctrinal du XIe au XIVe Siècle* (Paris, 1956); G. de Lagarde, *La Naissance de l'Esprit Laique,* 5 vols. (Paris, 1956–63); W. and A. Kneale, *The Development of Logic* (Oxford, 1966); F. Van Steenberghen, *Aristotle in the West* (Louvain, 1955); P. Vignaux, *Justification et Prédestination au 14e siècle* (Paris, 1934); P. Vignaux, "Nominalisme," *Dictionnaire de Théologie Catholique* (Paris, 1931), 11: 717–84. J. R. Weinberg, *A Short History of Medieval Philosophy* (Princeton, 1964).

tions of a preordained harmony between what was in the mind and what really existed. For all the diversity with which, from the time of Abelard (1079–1143) at least, the precise nature of reality and the mind's capacity to grasp it had been interpreted, the great majority of twelfth- and thirteenth-century thinkers proceeded from the rapport between them. Since the mind forms universal concepts, which, however they originate, can remain indifferent to and independent of actually subsisting individuals, the overwhelming tendency was to interpret reality in terms of universal natures or essences or forms as the created expression of the universal archetypes or divine ideas in God. That held whether the particular inspiration of a thinker was Neoplatonist or Aristotelian.

In retrospect this community seems more significant than many of the commonly regarded doctrinal differences which, although real enough, tend to be exaggerated largely because of the exaggerated stress put upon antecedents and pedigrees in what too often passes for the history of ideas. Thus the central disputes of the middle and later thirteenth century over such issues as a plurality of forms, the principle of individuation, the soul's conjunction with a corporeal body, illumination of the soul versus abstraction from the images left by the senses as the source of knowledge, shared certain basic suppositions: that forms are the determinants of being; that individual natures are derived from universal natures; that the soul is a spiritual being; that truth is of universal essences or natures; and that individuals owe their intelligibility to them. How they were conceived was therefore secondary, burning though the differences could be. For whether the soul is considered simply in relation to itself as a self-subsisting spiritual being or in relation to the body as its form, and whether the universal natures constituting whatever exists can be known immediately in the soul by its own inner light or only by abstraction from individuals experienced first by the senses, the spirituality of the soul and the universality of the essences, at once constituting being and knowledge of it, are assumed. Consequently to separate concepts of essence and existence and to identify each with different outlooks, as the hallmarks of Augustinianism and Thomism respectively, is artificial for it confuses what are merely different interpretations of essence as either synonymous with existence or, from an Aristotelian standpoint, as only realized or actualized in existence. The difference that is to say is as modes of being, not different kinds of being.

That can equally be said of what is known by either illumination or abstraction; while the two modes of knowledge are fundamentally antithetical and can be legitimately regarded as the touchstone of the difference between an Augustinian and Aristotelian epistemology before the coming of Duns Scotus (d. 1308) and Ockham (d. 1349), the object of both kinds of knowledge was the universal. Hence they were different, if also opposed, routes to the same destination.

Now it was just this community of assumptions that broke down in the fourteenth century. It was succeeded by a new pluralism and new alignments. That did not happen all at once; already in the last two decades of the thirteenth century the metaphysical union of concepts and reality was under increasing scrutiny; and at least one thinker, Peter John Olivi (d. 1298), rejected it. At no time had it meant unanimity as the diversity of some of the doctrines just mentioned should indicate; while the proclamation of the self-sufficiency of natural reason by the so-called Latin Averroists in the 1260s and 1270s, before their condemnation in 1277, was a more direct challenge to a Christian outlook than anything in the fourteenth century. The Latin Averroists, however, represented the negation of a Christian framework at all, hence their suppression. The re-orientation that came with the fourteenth century on the other hand was precisely through redefining that framework above all in its foundations of being, knowledge, and belief. It therefore, as we have already said, represented a shift back to first principles, which changed the character of subsequent thought.

To begin with it signified the end of system. After Duns Scotus and more than anyone Ockham, there were—with the possible exception of Nicholas of Cusa in the fifteenth century—no further attempts to order the whole of reality within the comprehensive systems so characteristic of thirteenth-century thinkers like Albert the Great, Bonaventure, Thomas Aquinas, Henry of Ghent, and many others. The search for understanding moved from metaphysics to evidence, and speculation from an independent world of abstractions to concrete meanings in the real world. At first sight the change appears merely negative and unconstructive; even today it tends to be interpreted largely as one of intellectual decline and loss of direction. Certainly from the second two decades of the fourteenth century not a great deal that was formative remained of the thirteenth-century achievement and there was no attempt to replace the edifices that had stood before by anything comparable. From that aspect there was decline, in the dissolution of what had previously existed. But soaring intellectual cathedrals to which the thirteenth-century systems have sometimes been likened can also from another perspective seem more like castles in the air, and loss of direction more a change of direction. Then such displacement can also be seen as an achievement whatever the form it takes.

The intellectual developments of the fourteenth century share this double perspective. There was an overall loss of coherence through a loss of continuity and the interruption of the previous lines of development. But there was also a new coherence in detail that came with a new autonomy of inquiry. Both were the accompaniments of the separation of the conceptual from the real, which was the great new intellectual fact of the fourteenth century. It was by no means universal. Yet as the dominant tendency, which derived from Ockham's denial of an independent conceptual order of reality, opposing outlooks were defined in relation to it: most sharply in the polarity between the New Way *(Via Moderna)* of the Ockhamists and the Old Way *(Via Antiqua)* of varying forms of tradition. That division, however, masks as much as it reveals. As we have already said there were not only new alignments but a new pluralism, which in its scientific aspects might almost be called a positivism. It is striking that greater advances were made in the fourteenth century in mathematics, physical theory, and logic than at any other time in the Middle Ages before or after—that is to say in the interval between the abandonment of the embracing systems to which all knowledge had tended to be subordinated and the congealing in the fifteenth century of the new conceptions which had succeeded the older ones in the fourteenth century. Although the independent development of these and other branches of knowledge goes back in some cases—notably logic—to the twelfth century they attained a new identity in the fourteenth century, particularly through the appearance of the scientific schools at Oxford and Paris. It was then that the main problems, theories, and solutions were largely defined for the next two centuries. Moreover, hardly less striking, they were to a great extent pursued independently of the theological and philosophical questions from which they had mostly originated, having their own modes of expression and literary forms in the different kinds of treatises on proportions, calculations, and logical *sophismata*. While many of the leading figures, such as Bradwardine, Buridan, and Nicholas of Oresme were also philosophers or theologians or ecclesiastics, or all three, many seem to have devoted themselves wholly to scientific or logical problems: a new departure, even if as we shall consider in the third part, science was itself then nearer to philosophy of science than modern science as the direct study of natural phenomena. Finally, the absence among those engaged in such activities of any exclusive doctrinal allegiance, and sometimes of any discernible allegiance at all, is perhaps the best indication of the intellectual fluidity of the period. It made for a new openness which complemented the loss of system involved in the redrawing of conceptual boundaries.

So did the redrawing of those boundaries. If anything may be said to distinguish the fourteenth century intellectually it is, as I have already mentioned, the preoccupation with the divergent conditions of natural knowledge and revealed truth. From having been prolegomena they became independent pursuits, largely transforming philosophical and theological discourse in the process. From the time of Ockham, questions were treated less for their own immediate import than to exhibit their logical, epistemological, and theological implications. Understanding and knowledge were thus subordinated to, or more properly subsumed under, the formal requisites of meaning and evidence. They became the main focus of philosophical and theological debate in the middle decades of the fourteenth century and of the new alignments which were largely defined by reference to them. Although, as we shall see, there was no hard and fast line of demarcation between the Old and the New Ways there were three principal areas of dispute where their differences were expressed.

The first and the one that more obviously than any other determined their division was over the nature of what was known and the source of knowledge. It was inaugurated by Ockham's identification of both with individual things existing outside the mind, which he took for the sole ontological reality. It should become clear in the next chapter that in Ockham's case much more was involved than merely denying the independent existence of universals. That became the hallmark of the *Via Moderna* in the fifteenth century, making it indistinguishable from Nominalism. Its immediate effect however in the fourteenth century was to introduce an asymmetry between the conceptual and the real and to recast the notion of reality in its light. Universal knowledge was not denied; but in Ockham's view it could only be reached through knowledge of individuals and it was ultimately about individuals. It was that which reversed the accepted order. From attempting to explain the place of individuals in a world of universal natures and essences, the problem was henceforth to account for universals in an exclusively individual world. It led to the substitution of a logical for a metaphysical order, with universals treated solely as concepts whose meaning depended upon the grammatical form and logical signification of the terms standing for them, as we shall consider. In consequence, the diversity previously ascribed to being—as individual, universal, essence, existence—was transposed to the diversity of terms—abstract, concrete, absolute, connotative—representing the same individual being diversely. With that went the restriction of actual knowledge to what could be known immediately as actually existing; hence the existence of one thing could not be known or inferred from the existence of another. By the doctrine of individual knowledge, then, evident knowledge was of what could be known to exist, and nothing else.

That leads us to the other two areas of certainty and uncertainty in knowledge and belief. If the scope of evident knowledge was restricted to knowledge of actual existence, so by the same token was its efficacy. But whereas there were many who opposed the Ockhamist conception of individual knowledge, the belief in the inherent uncertainty and contingency of all existence, other than God's, was a tenet common to all Christians. Its widespread explicit acknowledgment by the majority of thinkers in the period from the 1320s to the 1360s is among the most significant of these new developments. It affected knowledge and belief alike; in neither did it imply an Ockhamist standpoint. The almost universal tendency to imagine that it did is the greatest single misconception still prevalent about the thought of the fourteenth and indeed fifteenth centuries. It has been responsible for confusing Ockhamism with the doctrine of uncertainty and both with Nominalism, while ignoring the same tendencies among those who were neither Ockhamists nor Nominalists (as Ockham himself was not). The label of Nominalism, whatever its justification in the limited and barren philosophical context of the fifteenth and the sixteenth centuries, when the earlier intellectual vitality had been spent, lies like a pall— recently renewed—across the philosophy and theology of the fourteenth century. It overrides the heterogeneity which is its most notable aspect and is expressed in the very eclecticism of the period compared with the previous epoch as the measure of their discontinuity. There was a new critical awareness in the fourteenth century from which scarcely a thinker was immune. Thus the same thinker could, like Gregory of Rimini, combine a traditional Augustinian theology with an Ockhamist epistemology of external, but not internal, knowledge, and yet also invoke God's omnipotence to suspend the normal workings of both nature and grace; or like Nicholas of Autrecourt go beyond Ockham in the ultimate limits imposed upon certainty without apparently upholding Ockham's doctrine of individual knowledge or involving himself in the theological implications of uncertainty; or like John Buridan not even seek, as Ockham sought, to reconcile words with things and yet oppose Autrecourt and eschew theological speculation for scientific inquiry, where he employed non-Ockhamist conceptions. These and many other examples testify to the criss-crossing of conventional boundaries which defies simple classifications.

So far as both knowledge and belief were concerned there were two considerations. On the one hand, since only God is necessary, knowledge of all other existence than his, which in itself is unknowable, cannot be necessary knowledge or enter into demonstrations giving necessary knowledge. On the other hand since God as creator has freely willed the existence of everything, he could as freely in his omnipotence not have willed what he has created or have created or conserved it in some other way. Hence from the standpoints of both creation and creator, existence and its modes could have been different and thus also the certainty of knowledge and belief about them. They all shared the inherent contingency of creation, so that however necessary the laws that God had ordained for this world were, they were only conditionally necessary on God's having willed them and not by any unqualified absolute necessity of their own.

There was, as we have just remarked, nothing new in that; it was fundamental to the very notion of a Christian God; and had from the time of St. Augustine, in his doctrine of grace and predestination, been at the center of Western Christian tradition, periodically renewed in the teachings of Peter Damian (d. 1074) and St. Anselm (d. 1109) on divine omnipotence. But in the subsequent two centuries it had largely remained dormant as a formative influence until the last two decades of the thirteenth century, when it was revived first by Henry of Ghent (d. 1294) and then in the form which it was to take in the fourteenth century by Duns Scotus, in the distinction between God's two kinds of power: his ordained power *(potentia ordinata)* as his law for this world and his absolute power *(potentia absoluta)* as his omnipotence pure and simple, regarded solely in itself and expressed in the creed of an omnipotent God limited by nothing save logical self-contradiction, which would impair his power. As such it received its currency from Ockham, but in a use, as we have said, not exclusive to Ockhamism. Nor invariably as an explicit invocation of God's omnipotence.

Here, too, more was involved than the so-called dialectic between God's two kinds of power, or rather facets of the same power; it extended to a universal antinomy between the actual and the possible within knowledge itself as well as in nature and revelation. In the case of knowledge that did not for the most part entail direct recourse to God's omnipotence since it arose from the very limitations of existential knowledge. These had always been accepted; once more, the difference was that the means sought to transcend them were no longer metaphysical—through illumination or abstraction of extra-existential essences—but logical in the search for necessary propositions and demonstrations. That led to a narrowing of what could be known necessarily and certainly, with the extreme reached by Nicholas of Autrecourt's reduction of certainty to the principle of contradiction: that the same proposition cannot at once be both affirmed and denied; everything else was merely probable, including the idea of cause. Even for the majority who did not go so far, probability replaced necessity as the status of most propositions, while certainty, even of internal states, was contingent upon God's will.

This shift has commonly been regarded as the coming of an attitude of criticism and skepticism which destroyed the scholastic achievement. Critical indeed it was; but skeptical only in the context of previous certainties. Toward knowledge itself no one, including Nicholas of Autrecourt, doubted either the existence or knowledge of what could be known: it was their certainty that was denied, and with it their demonstrability, because of the contingency of creation. Illusions derived not—as they did for Hume —from the discrepancy between mental associations and reality, but, if at all, in those having the use of reason, from God's power to induce them as a token of his omnipotence. The source of uncertainty was therefore ontological not psychological, although in both cases it could only be overcome logically. As we shall consider, that meant transcending the mode of existence for the mode of possibility to reach self-evident, analytic propositions removed from any dependence upon contingent circumstances.

Consequently, we must distinguish between cause and effect. The systematic exploration of what could be known in a contingent world introduced a new analytical, above all logical, sophistication. Far from grinding all meaning into a fine logical dust it brought liberation from the maze of speculations and distinctions in which meaning had become enveloped. That the same new modes created in time their no less constricting cocoon of distinctions and speculations does not detract from the initial effect of cutting a way through the conceptual and often fanciful to the real. For the first time in the Middle Ages the enterprise of attempting to explain the use of general terms and concepts by their direct resonance with being and its properties was virtually abandoned. Once the exclusively individual nature of existence or the unattainability of universal being was accepted, the world became at once a more knowable and a less perplexing place. The ingenuity that had for so long been expended upon reconciling individuals with their universal natures could instead be redirected to exhibiting the ways in which singular things can be described by universal words: what had been a problem—virtually insoluble—of the nature of being, became a problem of language. It was now recognized as such. That is the magnitude of the change from the diversity of being to the diversity of terms describing it. The previous order was thus reversed. The direct rapport between experience and individual existence and the indirect correspondence—or lack of inherent correspondence—between many words and reality replaced the direct correspondence of substantive words with being and the indirect relation of experience to universal reality. The asymmetry was henceforth between concepts and individual existence where before it had been between universal and individual being. The latter now became the regulator instead of the concepts which transcended it.

The paradox, in the light of the received view of the fourteenth century, is that the change denotes an almost naive confidence in the intelligibility of the world and the capacity of reason to discern it. It inaugurated a new path of inquiry which, greatly modified, was ultimately to be vindicated in subsequent developments, both scientific and logical. But in the context of the fourteenth century it could only be destructive of the existing modes without being comprehensive enough to substitute a new outlook. The ultimate framework provided by a Christian conception of reality remained unmodified; the modification was of its secondary characteristics, in the interpretations of that conception, expressed in the different schools and systems of thought. The changed basis of meaning and evidence was too slender to support the metaphysical and theological superstructures of the immediate past.

That is to be seen above all in the effects upon theology, the third area of contention, and at the time the one most crucial. There was a virtual abandonment of a systematic attempt at a natural theology in the thirteenth-century sense of finding natural reasons for revealed truths. Instead the stress was upon their natural unknowability and dependence upon God's will. In both these respects the attitude to theology was an extension of that toward knowledge: only what could be known to exist was evident and nothing that existed apart from God was necessary or in itself certain. Applied to theology that meant there could be neither evident nor necessary knowledge of its truths accessible to reason. On the one hand those that could be conceived naturally, such as God's existence, were inevident; on the other those that were beyond reason's comprehension such as God's triunity or the Incarnation or predestination could not be even conceived naturally. From both aspects, therefore, theology lacked the requisites of knowledge in the proper sense *(scientia)*. It presupposed faith, the possession of which was exclusive to Christians through baptism and the other sacraments. Reason's role was thus restricted to elucidating the meaning and the implications of revealed truth. That had two consequences.

First, from the standpoint of natural reason, there were no longer necessary or demonstrative theological truths; at most they were probable; while truths such as those of the Trinity, or God's power to foresee future actions which are freely willed, contradicted reason and logic. The interest in exploring such problems was frequently a logical one of seeking to resolve apparently insoluble paradoxes; that included theological propositions especially framed to test logical wit such as that condemned at Paris in 1340 that "God and creature are nothing" where the object was to distinguish the different senses of "nothing." At first sight the lapse into a kind of logicizing theology which follows Ockham's break with many of the accepted theological solutions, though as we shall see in the second chapter his own were theologically impeccable, appears frivolous, or blasphemous, or indeed both. That is how it has for long been regarded. Recent closer examination of the context of some of the opinions makes that view less obvious. If their purport was logical it was such by the logic of revealed truth. That is their difference from the past. Where before many theological propositions, held on faith, had been treated as conclusions to be reached by reason, in the fourteenth century they tended increasingly to become premises, held only on faith, from which further conclusions could be drawn. Thus, reason could not display the certainty or often even the probability of revelation, merely the implications which could be shown to follow from its articles. According to how far they were taken they could become extravagant or inimical to faith.

That brings us to the second consequence. Many of the paradoxes were from invoking God's absolute power to modify or supersede the existing dispensation which he had ordained. That for the most part took the form of dispensing with intermediary second causes so that he could do directly what he normally did through created agents. Alternatively, he could entirely reverse the prevailing order and enable someone or something to do the opposite of what was naturally possible, especially in gaining the reward of eternal life.

The combination of the logic of revealed truth with the logic of its contingency, expressed in divine omnipotence, largely changed the forms of theological discourse in the fourteenth century. To begin with, it made theology at once certain and uncertain. As a body of beliefs held by faith it was indubitable with a certainty denied to most knowledge and of a kind which made it independent of all knowledge. But as including truths of what God had freely willed—as well as revealed—it could also be transcended in the name of the supreme truth of God's omnipotence, while the manifest incomprehensibility of many of its truths left them open, from the standpoint of reason, to opposing dialectical interpretations. Hence the certainty of belief as a whole was mediated by the uncertainty of possible or probable alternatives in particular. They monopolized the attention for much of the fourteenth century and beyond. They principally concerned God's relation to what was outside him, although the logical problems connected with reconciling the oneness of God's essence with the trinity of divine persons remained a perennial topic. That does not, however, mean that they were all of the same kind.

Here we again come against the received view—recently restated—of a nominalist theology.[3] The term like any other is an arbitrary one which must be a matter of choice provided it does not claim too much. Now since "Nominalist" is a philosophical label which carries a definite epistemological meaning, a nominalist theology should imply the same epistemology or at least that its upholders were Nominalists. In fact it does neither, nor is it intended as such. It denotes instead the interplay between God's ordained and absolute power, above all over questions of moral theology: justification, predestination, merit, free will, and sin. These undeniably constitute some of the central theological issues in the fourteenth century and they are in a direct line of descent to Reformation theology via nominalists like Peter d'Ailly and Gabriel Biel. Moreover they largely operated by means of the so-called dialectic between God's two kinds of power. But, as in the application of the word "Nominalism" to philosophy, that was far from representing the whole of theology at the time or exclusive to those who shared an Ockhamist standpoint. No less prominent in the middle and later decades of the fourteenth century was the problem of free will's capacity to act not only virtuously but also freely. Here one of the burning issues—quite as prominent as those over grace and predestination—was that mentioned earlier of the relation of God's foreknowledge to free will's future actions. It did not ordinarily involve juxtaposing God's two kinds of power but reconciling two different theological truths: that God has eternal infallible knowledge of everything, past, present, and future; and that man's will is free. Nor again did the form in which it came to be posed derive from Ockham who had expressly eschewed the attempt to explain such a mystery. That, however, did not prevent both his adherents and opponents from doing so in those very terms.

The New Way in theology, then, as in philosophy, cannot be seen as the preserve of a particular outlook or school. Each was less an identifiable set of tenets than a refocusing upon problems raised by the contingency of

3. The latest and most comprehensive restatement of the thesis of a Nominalist theology is by H. A. Oberman, *The Harvest of Medieval Theology* (Cambridge, Mass., 1963).

creation for natural and supernatural certainty. If the effect was to delimit one from the other more sharply than before, making them virtually independent, it was also to bring the same attitudes and modes of reasoning to bear upon both. There was a common dialectical approach in the probing of received truths, which, particularly among Ockham's immediate successors in 1330s and 1340s, was frequently carried to the point where theology passed into dialectic, as in the conclusions over God's power to cause sin, to which we shall refer in the second chapter.

That was the other, negative, side of the New Way: the pursuit of argument, often to the limits of extreme paradox, tended to displace the search for substantive meaning; and concern with the conditions of certainty only succeeded in producing greater uncertainty. The outcome for philosophy and theology by the mid-fourteenth century was a widespread loss of speculative nerve. With only a few exceptions the substantive problems were largely forsaken for dialectical ones or given dialectical solutions; the inventiveness formerly devoted to new concepts was now reserved for the dissection of old ones. Conceptual fertility was followed by terminological luxuriance, where the formal aspects of discourse now proliferated in the different senses words and propositions could have. The new windows opened by Ockham also opened the way to the sterile cavilling that exclusive concern with formal meaning for its own sake must always bring to philosophy and in this case to theology as well. Compared with the thirteenth century, the result was disequilibrium. The central terrain of both philosophy and theology was largely abandoned, leaving behind pockets of predominantly dialectical activity, while most of the constructive intellectual energies gravitated to what had been the peripheries, of logic and scientific enquiry, with a new widespread concern for spirituality and the quality of Christian life. Although many thinkers occupied more than one of these regions, there was, as we have said before, a growing number who devoted themselves solely to logic, science, or spirituality without defined theological or philosophical positions, or indeed interests. That these, too, largely ended in a similar impasse by the middle of the fifteenth century was due to the same failure to go beyond the existing presuppositions. For all the stress upon analysis and experience, the cast of thinking was still predominantly speculative, within a framework of Christian and, where nature and logic were concerned, Aristotelian conceptions. So long as these prevailed, neither thinking nor knowledge could attain new ways of conceiving reality; they were therefore bound to move within the existing channels, widening and deepening them, and periodically breaching them without overflowing into a new configuration. Not until there was emancipation from the old qualitative categories together with new quantitative methods of measurement and calculation was that possible in science, while philosophy waited upon correspondingly new conceptions once it had effectively abdicated from attempting to uphold those which depended upon revealed truth and involved assumptions inaccessible to natural reason. That in turn impaired the efficacy of logic in being caught up in the sterilities of later scholasticism: it needed the new mathematical and symbolic approach of the nineteenth and twentieth centuries to restore the line of development lost in the fifteenth and sixteenth centuries. Each of these different branches therefore was fettered by the limits of the outlook it subserved, just as the impulse toward spirituality was frustrated by the institutional failure of the church at the same time. How they were resolved or indeed whether, apart from the problems of science, they were ever resolved, lies outside the scope of this book: save only to remark that in the same way as they were not from a sudden breakdown of an entire outlook they were not simultaneously transcended in some new resolution.

That takes us back to our starting point. The change of outlook we have been discussing was from reinterpreting the accepted view of the world; it was not from a new view of the world. The immediate challenge was therefore to previous interpretations. But the very process of attempting to make sense of the common presuppositions—whether Christian or Aristotelian—led further away from that world view, until it was no longer adequate to support the conclusions being drawn from revealed truth or nature. The scale of the change should not be exaggerated during the period with which we are concerned; it did not mean the appearance of modern modes of thinking or science. Nor, even more germane, did it imply any flight from the accepted beliefs; indeed, not until the nineteenth century did the separation of natural and supernatural truth, which was the principal consequence of the breakdown of the medieval outlook, issue in comprehensive non-Christian conceptions of the whole of reality, as opposed to separate philosophies and scientific theories which did not depend upon Christian principles. In the fourteenth century much of the intellectual activity was directed precisely to saving the appearances of Christian and Aristotelian doctrines. For the thinkers of the time it was not they who were breaking with the past; rather they were restoring it from the interposition of the recent past. Ockham's quarrel lay almost exclusively with the "moderns" of the previous fifty years, as in a less radical way Duns Scotus's had done so as well. Not until Nicholas of Cusa (1404–64), almost a hundred years after the high point of Ockhamism, in the 1340s and 1350s, did a Christian thinker north of the Alps—with the possible exception of Nicholas of Autrecourt—completely break with the entire basis of scholasticism, which by then was contracting into the separate warring schools of Nominalism and the revived forms of Thomism, Scotism, and Albertism.

What, then, does this turning away from the systems of the thirteenth century denote? The keynote is disengagement: of concepts from reality, of natural reason from what cannot be known naturally, of belief from the limits of what has been ordained. It operated on the two planes of what we may call the epistemological and the positivist, the first involving a new awareness of the conditions regulating knowledge and belief and the relation between them; the second the physical nature of the world and what can be known generally. They were not necessarily connected: as we have seen, one of the novelties of the situation was the tendency to pursue each independently in its own terms.

There has been no lack of interpretations either of the nature of the change or its significance. At one time it was widely seen as the beginning of a modern outlook both in philosophy and in theology, with the stress upon individual existence and experience, and in science with its movement toward a quantitative treatment of natural phenomena. Today, judgment is more qualified; but the tendency persists of treating the fourteenth century as some kind of watershed between a medieval and post-medieval outlook and to seek the origins in the Paris condemnations of 1277. Let us consider each in turn.

So far as the first is concerned from what has already been said it must follow that the fourteenth century was an intellectual watershed. But of what? Individualism? Freedom of enquiry? A new scientific, "objective" attitude?—the most commonly attributed characteristics. Not if what has already been said is accepted. None of these was noticeably more or less present before than after. To take them as the criteria of the difference between a medieval and a post-medieval outlook is to commit a fallacy of accident in confusing quite distinct considerations. Individualism, the most ubiquitous of the traits commonly attributed to post-medieval man, has not, it may be observed, until now been mentioned once in the preceding pages. Not wholly by accident. The individualism that interested Ockham —with whom its introduction is frequently associated—was that of the singular as the unit of existence; its extension to man was merely an aspect of that conviction, whether applied to human experience or human society, each only consisting of individuals; and when it involved God's power to reward an act of free will directly, without the preceding need for grace, that had nothing at all to do with an individual's own worth, but only with God's power to dispense with second causes: a qualification of individuality in the light of God's omnipotence, which far from representing a new conception of individualism, heightens the accepted Christian view.

The so-called discovery of the individual begins—if, with such individualists as many of the early Christian fathers, it can be said to begin at all —with St. Augustine's exploration of the soul; if it lay dormant until the eleventh century, it is enshrined in the Christian belief in an immortal individual soul, the affirmation of which, as we shall mention shortly, was more than anything the catalyst of the Paris condemnations of 1277. Certainly from the twelfth century onward, awareness of the individual, in the mystic's search for God within the soul and in the emulation of Christ in the world, was central to spiritual and religious consciousness. But it was not the individualism of self-consciousness that we have inherited from the humanists of fourteenth- and fifteenth-century Italy. That is where the developments we are considering differed from those of contemporary Italian humanism. Within the medieval tradition the individual was the measure of nothing taken for himself; he owed his meaning to God; and awareness of self must be transcended by awareness of God. That was only accentuated in the fourteenth and fifteenth centuries both in the theology of God's absolute power and in the spirituality of the individual's direct rapport with God, whether through mystical union or God's word revealed in the Bible. Their individuality was of an individual soul with its creator. The casuality was the universalism of intermediaries—the sacraments, the church hierarchy, the laws of men, as well as the universal essences, which were the bearers of existence. It was from these that the individual sought emancipation. But in the name of his direct dependence upon God, in which he remained—to say nothing of new intermediaries—when it was achieved. Centuries were to elapse before man took the title of his own master. Hence it has no part in the breakdown of the medieval outlook.

Much the same can be said of the other suggested attributes. They belong to different contexts which permit no direct comparison. Galileo's recantation before the Inquisition in 1633 happened over three hundred years after Ockham's death (not at the hands of the Inquisition). If the events of 1633 were the coda to five hundred years of periodic attempts at thought control, the thought that prompted them on that occasion was itself the outcome of centuries of scientific inquiry, for the most part impeded less by any direct intervention from on high than by its own absolute presuppositions. As we have suggested, the framework they constitute controls any system, open or closed. What distinguished the outlook of the Middle Ages from a modern outlook was the impermissibility of conceiving alternative—i.e., non-Christian, non-geocentric presuppositions about the nature of reality. Submission to those rather than to the dictates of natural reason and experience as the final arbiter made it a closed outlook. But that did not mean closed minds. There was an unbroken line of thinkers from the twelfth century to Galileo—the final victim of the system—who evinced precisely all those qualities of intellectual rigor and natural curiosity which are taken as the hallmark of a scientific approach. Hence the change was not so much in personal attitudes to knowledge—dogmatism did not end with the Middle Ages—as in the scope allowed to enquiry. The further removed it was from impinging upon revealed truth, the more independent it could be: it was that which allowed the uninterrupted development of logic and the different branches of knowledge for most of the time. The achievement of the fourteenth century was to take that independence to the furthest limits compatible with a Christian outlook. The means of doing so was precisely the disengagement of one from the other as already described. It is there above all that its significance is to be gauged. The testimony is in the very developments in theology and knowledge to which the new movements of the sixteenth century, regardless of their beneficence or otherwise, were heir. In that sense the fourteenth century can be regarded as a watershed between the medieval and the nonmedieval. What precipitated it?

Here we come to the condemnations of 1277. First we should distinguish between treating them as a catalyst in the rethinking that becomes apparent in the last two decades of the thirteenth century and making them first cause of the subsequent change in outlook. Superficially it may seem to explain more by invoking what appears to be a cause—a temptation which it has become fashionable to indulge rather than resist. More often than not it results merely in jejune reduction to antecedents that explain nothing beyond the sequence in which a set of events has occurred; but a temporal order is not necessarily a causal order. To say that the Paris condemnations precipitated the change in outlook that began in the thirteenth century and *therefore* they were the cause of the way in which Duns Scotus and so Ockham and their followers and opponents thought, would be to deny the very differences between them which are due to individual agency. The relation of the Paris condemnations to what followed could only be of the form "If C, then E^1, E^2, E^3 . . ." if all subsequent thinking was assimilable to the same modes and expressed in the same terms as those in the condemnations. Instead, we are confronted with an irreducible diversity of individual outlooks that were concerned with shifting problems, precisely through the emergence of new modes of thought: there is nothing in the 219 condemned propositions which can explain Duns Scotus's formal distinction or Ockham's notion of intuitive cognition; but both, on the other hand, become only fully intelligible within the context of problems from which they emerged. It is in that sense that the condemnations have a part in plotting the course of intellectual development to the fourteenth century, in the less omnicausal role of a necessary, as opposed to the sufficient, condition of subsequent developments.

We have already suggested the principal grounds for their importance. The condemnations of 1277 were a prohibition upon natural philosophy to reach conclusions which contradicted revealed truth. As such they amounted to the rejection of the independent naturalistic outlook which had emerged above all in the arts faculty at Paris university over the preceding thirty years. In itself there was nothing new in the hostility of the guardians of Christian faith—principally the theologians whether in the theological faculty of the universities or in the hierarchy of church— to the encroachments of philosophy; it was inherent in the very tension between what could be known from reason and natural experience and what must be believed; and it had erupted in condemnations and bans long before those of 1270 and 1277. The difference was in the latter's comprehensiveness and, in retrospect, finality. They signaled the effective end of an independent realm of philosophy in matters which belonged to theology: that is to say, in all that concerned the world as God's creation and his role as creator. It marked the beginning of philosophy's circumscription, bounded on the one hand by the demands of faith and on the other by the growing recognition of the limits of natural reason which put revealed truth beyond its reach. The result was a progressive narrowing of the area of philosophical enquiry and a new preoccupation with what could be known by both faith and reason, which led to redefining their relation and the certainty they could give.

The role of the condemnations in this development is that they provided the orientation, or more accurately it came from the reaction to them. The explanation is to be seen in the doctrines condemned. They arose from the new body of Aristotelian and Neoplatonist philosophy, which had been introduced into Western Europe during the twelfth century through the gradual translation of most of Aristotle's works, together with those of his Arabian and Jewish commentators who had evolved their own independent systems through combining Aristotelian and Neoplatonic ideas mainly—until Averroës (d. 1198)—in the mistaken belief that they were all from Aristotle. By the beginning of the thirteenth century Christian thinkers in the West, who had hitherto derived most of their philosophical concepts from Aristotle's logic and a handful of mainly Neoplatonist texts, were now confronted with a full-fledged natural cosmology, which explained the world in non-Christian terms. It presented a direct challenge to a Christian interpretation. Instead of God as the immediate creator and conserver of the universe, who had freely brought it into existence and governed it by his providence, and of man's special place within it, next to the angels, in possessing an immortal spiritual soul, God became merely an indirect first mover who did no more than set in motion an eternal procession of cause and effect with no immediate involvement in its operations. On this view the world was eternal and man was subject to the heavenly bodies: personal immortality, free will, and individual salvation vanished. Such was the threat presented by the new doctrines at the theological level.

That is not to say that they were immediately uppermost; on the contrary, they were implications which only gradually came to assume importance with the emergence of an independent, predominantly Aristotelian, school of philosophers in the arts faculty at Paris in the 1260s and 1270s. By then Averroës, Aristotle's most authoritative commentator for the West, seems to have been the dominant influence. Even so it is difficult to know how far they carried their ideas: condemned articles are usually a more reliable guide to the outlook of the condemners than the condemned. What concerns us here is that, after the initial opposition to the study of Aristotle and his commentators at Paris (other universities, notably Oxford and Toulouse, remained immune from such interference), Aristotle's writings had by the 1250s come to constitute the main part of the arts course, devoted to the study of the principal branches of profane—nontheological —knowledge. The transformation which they wrought is testimony to the disturbing presence of a non-Christian outlook, not upon knowledge itself —where, as we have already stressed, Aristotle's cosmology provided the foundation of scientific and natural enquiry—but upon Christian belief.

Until the thirteenth century the main philosophical, as opposed to logical or scientific, inspiration had been Neoplatonist, beginning with St. Augustine and culminating in the almost purely Platonic speculations of some of the leading thinkers commonly, if perhaps mistakenly, associated with the cathedral school of Chartres in the twelfth century. Although scarcely a thinker before Ockham did not draw upon Neoplatonist concepts in order to fashion some kind of Christian metaphysics, it was the coming of Aristotle in the thirteenth century as a philosopher—above all in his metaphysics, ethics, and philosophical aspects of his cosmology—which was principally responsible for the impasse which led to 1277. He presented a comprehensive non-Christian alternative, which, if it provided the philosophical sinews for a Christian outlook, also provided a nontranscendental interpretation of reality which was a negation of a Christian outlook. In that sense, the progressive deneoplatonizing of Aristotle, as more accurate translations of his works were made from the original Greek and the nonauthentic elements identified, accentuated the naturalistic nature of his philosophy, which its initial mélange with Neoplationist ideas had masked, and had made more assimilable to Christian conceptions.

It is accordingly misconceived to regard Aristotle's philosophy as the mainstay of medieval Christian philosophy: only St. Thomas Aquinas properly incorporated it into his system, and he suffered the stigma of having done so in the years immediately surrounding the condemnations. The unalloyed philosophical form in which Aristotelian ideas were held in the arts faculty at Paris, however, crystallized their latent opposition to Christian beliefs. Whether those who pursued Aristotle's concepts in their own terms did so simply in their capacity as teachers and taught, as expositors of ideas they did not themselves hold, or were themselves thoroughgoing Aristotelians, is now impossible to know; certainly they distinguished between conclusions arrived at philosophically and theological truths that must be accepted independently and regardless of philosophical reasoning. But that defense—often called "the double truth"—was brushed aside by their censors; they were condemned precisely for "exceeding the limits of their faculty," in taking philosophy where only faith could go.

As to the condemned opinions themselves, the themes were the same in 1270 as in 1277, and proscribed by the same person, Stephen Tempier, bishop of Paris, himself a former master in the theological faculty there. The difference was in their scale: thirteen in 1270; 219 in 1277 extending pell-mell to everything that sounded scandalous or suspicious.[4] They centered upon providence, the eternity of the world, creation, the immortality of the human soul, and human free will, and together constituted a comprehensive *philosophical* denial of Christian belief. That included God's nature as a Trinity (proposition 1), his role as creator (2, 4, 5, 43, 44, 48, 49, 55), his omnipotence (25, 29), and his omniscience (42). Instead—on purely philosophical grounds—he could be conceived only as a remote, i.e., indirect, first cause (43, 44, 55), with power over the world exercised by the heavenly spheres and separated intelligence of Aristotelian and Neoplatonic cosmology (56, 60, 67, 71, 72, 78). Man in turn was dependent upon the latter, not God (73, 74); unlike the Christian God, these heavenly bodies operated eternally and determinately without freedom or contingency themselves or for creatures (87, 90, 92, 94, 95, 98, 99, 107). There was no such thing as an individual human intellect or soul; all human understanding was due to a single separated intelligence—the active intellect—animating all men. This doctrine of monopsychism was the distinc-

4. Given in H. Denifle and E. Chatelain, eds., *Chartularium Universitatis Parisiensis* (Paris, 1889), 1: No. 473, 543–55.

tive contribution of Averroës to what was otherwise for the most part a syncretism of Aristotelian and Arabian doctrines. Averroës alone of Aristotle's Moslem commentators had denied man a separate intellect, annexing the immaterial knowledge acquired by an individual under the influence of the active intellect to the latter to whom it returned on death. It was that notion more than any other that had precipitated the attack upon the Aristotelians—known somewhat inexactly from their association with it as the Latin Averroists—in the arts faculty. In the decade or so within which the two condemnations fell, a succession of the most eminent theologians at Paris and elsewhere, including the two outstanding Christian Aristotelians of the time, Albert the Great and Thomas Aquinas, denounced the idea of a single active intellect for all mankind. It became the badge of heterodox Averroism. Moreover, the dependence of the human intellect upon the active intellect subjected man's will to his understanding so that "it was necessitated by knowledge as the beasts are by their appetites" (159; also 129, 133, 159, 160, 163–4, 194). There was no such thing as free will (194). The primacy of the intellect over the will, a doctrine held on quite other grounds by Aquinas, thereby itself became a burning issue in the decades after 1277, and St. Thomas's teachings on the subject were not only a center of contention but were included in a more limited censure at Oxford by a fellow Dominican, Robert of Kildwardby, as archbishop of Canterbury shortly after that at Paris in 1277.

The assertion of determinism runs like a thread through the 219 propositions. Not that they represented a coherent outlook. They were, as we have suggested, a jumble, apparently thrown together in some haste by a number of different compilers. They included an innocuous treatise on courtly love as well as scabrous ethical and moral views. But their total effect was a rejection of the basic tenets of Christian belief: God's power and freedom to create or to know his creatures and their—in the case of man—free actions and free will were denied; in their place was put the inexorability of the heavenly bodies which, interposed between God and the universe, effectively usurped his role—including even the power to create, if only sins, monsters, and their own forms in what was material (187, 188, 196) —without any of the attributes which made him supreme being and providence, to say nothing of his nature as a Trinity of persons informing man. Whether or not the propositions were garbled—as some no doubt were—

they henceforth stood as a warning of where philosophy, left to itself, could lead. The year 1277 effectively meant the end of unrestrained philosophical speculation in its own, and not a Christian, right.

The effects upon subsequent thinking are apparent in a number of respects. First and foremost they are to be seen in the affirmation of God's freedom and the contingency of creation expressed in his absolute power to do whatever is not contradictory. From the time of Duns Scotus the appeal to God's omnipotence became as central to Christian thought as determinism had been to the Greco-Arabian thought of the arts faculty. It completely reversed the latter's emphasis. On the one hand, only God was eternal and necessary; on the other, he was so free that he could dispense with everything else. It is noteworthy that initially at least—before it tended also to become a device to justify extreme paradoxes among some of Ockham's followers like Robert Holcot and Adam of Woodham—the stress by Duns Scotus and Ockham was precisely upon God's power to supersede intermediaries and to do directly what he ordinarily did by the second causes in the way mentioned earlier. In that sense, deliberately or otherwise, the invocation of God's absolute power was a direct riposte to the necessitarianism of intermediaries.

In the second place, as we have also seen, the emphasis upon the contingency of creation affected the status of knowledge, so that no knowledge which was of existence was necessary knowledge. Here, again, the certainties that were adduced from a necessitarian order by the Paris artists became with Duns Scotus and above all Ockham merely probabilities. The possibility, inherent in all creation, of nonexistence or a different mode of existence was complemented by the lack of certainty in what could be known of actual existence. The notion of causality itself, the foundation of all demonstrative knowledge, became with Ockham simply a datum of experience derived from observation, as we shall mention in the next chapter, and not itself a demonstrable or self-evident truth. Philosophy thus lost the main means of arguing from necessary reasons to necessary conclusions, which had enabled the philosophers at Paris to oppose Christian truth by their own truths.

That meant in the third place a reduction in what was knowable. Where the Parisians had said that God could not be a Trinity because triunity was incompatible with absolute simplicity (proposition 1), Christian thinkers—

who had always regarded such truths as mysteries, unknowable naturally—increasingly made such unknowability a postulate of theological and philosophical discourse. One of the features of subsequent discussion is the systematic consideration of the scope of natural knowledge precisely in relation to faith, as we have remarked before. There was a conscious attempt, found among others in both Scotus and Ockham, to delineate their boundaries in the light of the limits of both.

Finally, it was on that basis that many of the issues raised by the condemnations were treated in the ensuing years. Thus the denial to God in the condemned propositions of the attribute of infinity in either his nature or his actions, confining it to his duration, i.e., eternity (proposition 29), was met by Duns Scotus's, and in a more restricted sense Ockham's, affirmation that God was distinguished ontologically from everything else as infinite being from finite being. Infinity, far from being banished, became in the fourteenth century one of the foci of theological and scientific interest, an indication perhaps of the new awareness of possibility that came with a reassertion of the contingency of the universe. Again where the Parisian philosophers refused God the title of creator yet allowed it to the heavenly bodies, careful distinction was drawn by Christian thinkers like Ockham between the act of creation which was from nothing, and could only by definition be from God, and generation which was from pre-existing matter and belonged to created beings. There was again no comparison. Similarly against the Paris negation of God's omniscience and human free will, the great debates on future contingents in the fourteenth century began from the premise of the existence of each. In all these cases, to say nothing of divine omnipotence and the overriding contingency of all God's actions, discussion had its starting point from what were held to be theological truths, beyond demonstration and question; its object was not to disprove or dispute their certainty as matters of faith, but as we stated earlier to elucidate their implications and to establish what, if any, natural evidence there was for them. However frequently the judgment of "not certain" or "probable" or "possible" was returned it had no bearing upon their status as theological truths.

That is, of course, the fundamental difference from the so-called double truth of the Paris philosophers. They may or may not have meant it when they said that what they denied by reason they continued to believe as

Christians, and conversely. But they were nevertheless prepared to press reasoning derived from purely philosophical premises to the point of outright negation of theological premises, which is to say that they allowed them to conflict because they allowed philosophy—or more accurately Aristotle—the same scope as they accepted for theology. To them one was not more given than the other. That was tantamount to making Aristotle's authority equal to Christian revelation. The Paris philosophers were therefore operating from two different, and contrary, sets of suppositions. It is that which makes them alien and puts them outside the framework of a Christian outlook; and correspondingly it is that which helps to explain the redefinition of that framework by subsequent generations. Aristotle and Averroës were not themselves, unlike their Christian disciples at Paris, proscribed after 1277. They were and continued to be accepted as pagan and infidel philosophers whose strength and limits were as non-Christians who could be followed, because of their own endowments, as far as reason and natural experience could lead within the limits of this world but not beyond. The recognition of those limits and where they lay led fourteenth-century thinkers to recast Christian thought and remain Christians. They owed their awareness of those limits above all to the earlier failure to observe them, a failure that culminated in the dénouement of 1277. There, if anywhere, the importance of the Paris condemnations would seem to lie.

That completes the attempt to identify the nature of the intellectual change that occurred in the fourteenth century. It was in no sense a wholesale rejection of past assumptions or their transformation into a new postmedieval or quasi-modern outlook; but a rethinking within a common Christian framework of absolute presuppositions, which had held for over a millennium and were to continue for another two and, in some cases, three hundred years. The effect was nevertheless to give a new direction to medieval thought and also spirituality, which had as its outcome the supersession of the very presuppositions on which it had rested. We must now look more closely at the changes themselves.

II. Knowledge and Belief

From what has already been said it will be apparent that in the changes to both philosophy and theology during the fourteenth century Ockham was a central figure. He more than anyone formulated the new modes of discourse that largely changed the traditional ones, or at least displaced them by those which for the next century or more were to become the dominant ones. But it should also be apparent that he did not come unheralded. For over a quarter of a century preceding the appearance of his first major, and probably earliest, work, his Commentary on the *Sentences,* composed in about 1317, the tendencies he expressed were growing: namely, the simplification of knowledge and of being to individual existence, thereby excluding divine illumination, intelligible species, seminal forms, principles of individuation; a shifting of the criteria of necessary knowledge from metaphysics—natures—to logic—propositions and demonstrations; and a stress upon God's freedom toward both nature and grace. These were far from being systematically developed into a new school or outlook before Ockham; indeed, probably no phase of scholasticism, certainly in terms of our present knowledge, remains more confused than the events in the decades immediately each side of the year 1300. They present the appearance of an intellectual babel of discordant views, with virtually no lines of demarcation between the different schools such as those which in the two generations until 1277 had broadly distinguished Augustinians and Aristotelians. Like most storms, those of the 1270s left more to clear away than anything they may have cleared; the ensuing forty years, far from being a period of calm, were of seemingly endless reconsiderations with the members of the two main orders of Dominicans and Franciscans, from whom the majority of thinkers were drawn, divided among themselves as well as between each other. Virtually every aspect of philosophy and natural theology was involved, with what lasting effects— as opposed to the intrinsic interest of the ideas themselves—can only be seen in the light of the subsequent changes with which we are concerned.

For that purpose we can mention three thinkers, Duns Scotus, Durandus of St. Pourçain, and Peter Aureole, who each in different ways can be regarded as Ockham's precursors, the last two for a time also his contemporaries. Their very diversity from one another helps at the same time to make them representative of the intellectual climate in which Ockhamism emerged. Two, Duns and Aureole, were Franciscans yet they held diametrically opposed views on the process of cognition, the nature of being, and the role of God's absolute power over grace. The third, Durandus, was a Dominican who fell foul of his own order for not sufficiently conforming to the doctrines of St. Thomas Aquinas, from 1314 its official doctor; with Aureole, Durandus upheld the individual nature of cognition, denying the need for intelligible species in the intellect in order to grasp the true nature of things. But unlike Aureole, he regarded the universal as something real whose presence in individuals of the same nature was the reason for the intellect's ability to identify them as belonging to the same nature. Hence there was for Durandus a correspondence between the universal in the mind and in things, although it could be seized directly in the individuals themselves. This almost old-fashioned Augustinianism, which seems to have become current among certain Franciscan thinkers like Matthew of Aquasparta in the last two decades of the thirteenth century, was unaccompanied by any doctrine of divine illumination: indeed it went with an almost Ockhamist identification of the intellect's powers with its actions. Durandus also differed from Aureole in his interpretation of God's award of grace and his knowledge of future contingents, sharing the same view as Scotus over grace, that God could dispense with its created form, or habit, in accepting someone as meritorious and worthy of eternal life. We therefore have the spectacle of Aureole and Durandus being radical in opposite directions: Aureole in reducing all universals to the work of the intellect, with genera and species signifying only individuals of different degrees of similarity each known through an immediate concept; Durandus in upholding God's absolute power in the order of grace. Neither can be called an Ockhamist, still less a Nominalist; nor is there any evidence that Ockham adopted the views of either; and he expressly rejected Aureole's conceptualism. Nevertheless, together they came close to important elements in Ockham's own outlook, just as in different ways Peter John Olivi and Henry of Harclay did: the latter, as chancellor of Oxford University in the period immediately preceding Ockham's sojourn there, went as far as Ockham was to go in denying the real existence of anything other than singulars of which universals were merely the confused and indistinct representations.

That they point to the future, both in Ockham's direction and in some cases beyond, is perhaps indicated by two further instances. The first is Aureole's acknowledgment, on quite different grounds from Ockham's, that there can be actual—intuitive—knowledge of nonexistent things because God can without contradiction make what does not exist appear to exist: an early recognition of the problem of certainty and evidence which as we have said was so much to absorb fourteenth-century thinkers. Second there is the—at first sight—startling paradox that both thinkers base their view of God's future knowledge on assumptions which, though different, seem close to those condemned in 1277. For Durandus, God's knowledge of what is future and undetermined is contingent because he is not the direct and immediate cause of his creatures' actions and so these actions can occur freely and independently of him; for Aureole, such knowledge is contingent on the basis of the Aristotelian proposition that what is contingent and future cannot be known determinately; hence God cannot know necessarily what remains indeterminate. In fact, each of these was merely a novel way of attempting to reconcile, philosophically, truths that were accepted as theologically indubitable: namely, as we have said before, that God is omniscient and free will is free. They were thus among the first of what was to become one of the most prominent examples of redirecting philosophical enquiry to the elucidation of truths held on faith. For that reason, however far their implications might be taken—and neither Aureole nor Durandus went further than stating his own grounds for the conclusion that God has contingent knowledge of what is future—they sprang from the very affirmation of premises that had been denied in the 1270s. That is where the great difference between the two attitudes lies.

Now if Aureole and Durandus, for all the bearing of some of their ideas upon subsequent developments, remain largely peripheral figures—transitional in the proper sense of lacking sufficiently defined affiliations with either the old or the new—Duns Scotus is so distinctive that his thought constitutes a new phase in itself. Although he, too, has frequently been taken as a transition—between the outlook of the thirteenth and the fourteenth centuries—that in his case is quite inapposite because, like Ockham, he remained a living presence in the thinking of the rest of the Middle Ages. And in two main respects. On the one hand, his thought was largely the point of departure for Ockham's; on the other, it paradoxically became identified with the Old Way in reaction to Ockham's New Way.

Scotus in a very real sense stands at the parting of the ways. To him more than anyone may be attributed the beginning of the systematic rethinking of the foundations of knowledge and belief in the form in which it was to be both transcended and developed by Ockham and his successors. To that extent Scotus provided the context for Ockham's outlook; and it is their concern with fundamentally the same problems of what can be known within a contingent universe that makes them, despite their opposed casts of thought and conflicting roles in its development, joint agents in the outlook of the later Middle Ages.

Their differences as thinkers should become apparent. In general terms they may be said to have proceeded from opposite directions. Duns sought to guarantee the reality of the conceptual order; Ockham, the reality of what lay outside it. Hence, where Duns's entire tendency was to seek a metaphysical basis for all our concepts, Ockham's was to reduce them to an exclusively individual import: he disjoined where Duns conjoined, rejecting as unreal what could not be assimilated to individual existence while Duns incorporated into reality whatever could be conceived to exist. Their dispute was therefore essentially philosophical. Within a common set of theological presuppositions, which Ockham largely took over unaltered from Scotus, the questions at issue concerned the nature of being, its relation to our conceptions of it, and the means of arriving at certain knowledge. They were raised by theologians but answered philosophically; Duns principally by recourse to elaborate metaphysical analysis; Ockham by a no less intricate recourse to logic. Between them they effectively restored philosophy to reason's pursuit of the nature of existence in its own terms, with which it had begun its medieval career in the eleventh century before knowledge of existence had been divided between Aristotle and the demands of natural theology.

Not that it was now pursued in defiance of either: the days of flying in the face of authority ended in 1277. Rather, the very uncertainties which henceforth constituted the problems of philosophy arose from the very certainties of revealed truth. In that they parallel those over the physical world: the contingency of the universe as God's creation at once put no limits upon its possibilities and limits upon the attainment of natural certainty. Duns, if not the first to recognize the problem, was the first expressly to meet it, as we shall consider shortly. The riposte his solutions brought from Ockham initiated a new philosophical era. Much of their opposition centered upon the perennial question of universals: namely, of the status of general concepts and terms, which had lain dormant since the time of Abelard nearly two centuries earlier. The older fashion among students of medieval thought to characterize Scotus and Ockham as the renewers of the struggle between Realism and Nominalism, is, for all its palpable exaggerations, true to the extent that they revived the issue of universals in a purely philosophical form, as the relation of the general to the singular, where before it had largely been subsumed under theological considerations of divine ideas and the object of the intellect (which as a spiritual power must know what is only immaterial and universal). That did not make Scotus or Ockham less of a theologian than his predecessors; it made them only more aware as theologians of the distinction between what constituted a theological and what a philosophical matter. The re-emergence of an independent area of philosophical speculation went with a reduction in the number of revealed truths that could be known and, after Ockham, in a restriction of the area of purely theological discourse. Each was the accompaniment of the clearer demarcation between theology and philosophy, for which Scotus and Ockham were more than anyone else responsible in its subsequent form. It is within that wider framework of redefinition, which became with Ockham increasingly one of disengagement, that their activities and their relation to one another are best seen.

Beginning with Scotus, it is not too much to say that his thought—and the main source of opposition to it by Ockham—represents the summation of the deep-seated Platonism—or Neoplatonism—which had from the time of the early fathers, above all, so far as the West was concerned, St. Augustine, taken an almost unshakable hold upon the majority of subsequent Christian thinkers. There was a direct resonance between a Christian conception of being as deriving from the archetypes or essences of things in God, and a Neoplatonist identification of reality with a series of forms or natures emanating from the One as supreme form. Aristotle had, with the egregious exception of the Latin Averroists, only confirmed that tendency, partly because until the middle of the thirteenth century he was still mistakenly associated with certain influential Neoplatonist writings—especially the so-called *Liber de Causis* taken from *The Elements of Theology* of Proclus—wrongly ascribed to him; but equally because of his own unresolved Platonism. The first had had the effect of inspiring early attempts to reconcile Aristotelian and Platonic conceptions especially of the universe and man's place within it; the second of continuing to identify reality with essences or natures or forms, exemplified in Aristotle's theory of abstraction. Even when Aristotle's own ideas had come to be differentiated from those of Neoplatonism by the mid-thirteenth century, the pull of Neoplatonism continued almost undiminished until Ockham. Ockham's break with tradition was precisely to deny any separate identity to what could not be encountered individually. He thereby swept away the mesh of abstractions —of natures, forms, distinctions, quiddities—which had been invested with their own reality through hypostasizing concepts: that was the focus of his attack upon Duns Scotus. For the first time in the Middle Ages, except for the eleventh and twelfth century Nominalists, universals were no longer the bearers of ontological reality.

To the extent that they had always previously been regarded as such, the whole of preceding medieval metaphysical tradition before Ockham, had been irreducibly Neoplatonic regardless of what its modes had owed to Aristotle; for independently of the way in which the universal essences or natures constituting all things were known—by the inner illumination of the Augustinians or through abstraction from the individual beings in which they inhered according to Aristotle—the essences remained. It is therefore misconceived to draw too sharp a distinction between the Augustinian and Aristotelian notions of being, the one undifferentiated, the other differentiated into essence and existence. In the end it is the same conception of being as that which is in some manner greater than and beyond individual beings. And one of its most striking aspects, common to virtually all medieval thinkers before Scotus, and above all Ockham—with a handful of exceptions found mainly among the Franciscan, non-Aristotelian school in the later thirteenth century—was the denial of direct individual cognition to the intellect. That was based upon the belief—enshrined in Aristotle's axiom adopted by St. Thomas Aquinas—that the intellect knows universals, but the senses know individuals, for the reason already indicated, that the intellect as an immaterial being only knows what is immaterial. As understood by the majority of thinkers, that amounted to denying the intellect direct knowledge of individuals in the widespread belief that only knowledge of universals was proper to it. As we shall see it was this interpretation of universal knowledge, as opposed to the Aristotelian sense of that which is known through universal and necessary propositions constituting the only proper knowledge, which was rejected by Ockham and the so-called Nominalists. Although Ockham was to go further than Scotus in making direct knowledge of individuals the foundation of all universal knowledge, he followed Scotus both in his account of how the intellect attained individual knowledge and in his reversal, or at least reinterpretation, of Aristotle's axiom to mean that the intellect has knowledge equally of universals and singulars but the senses only of singulars: a classic example of the widespread medieval practice of saving a doctrine's "appearances" to legitimize departures from it, and a warning against taking a thinker's sources at their face value.

In upholding the reality of essences, then, Scotus was doing nothing new. Nor was he being more Platonist than Aquinas; and in his acceptance of direct individual cognition by the intellect appreciably less Platonist. The relative proportions of Plato or Aristotle or any other influence upon him —in this case Avicenna or Henry of Ghent—are not, however, the terms in which to assess Scotus or any original thinker; for beyond anything he may owe to them his distinctiveness must be in what is from him, not from others, even if it is only to give a new import to old ideas. Shuffling antecedents will not measure what is new, and is more likely to obscure it.

No brief digest will do justice to any complex intellectual system, and that of Scotus is among the most complex of the Middle Ages or any age. In the context of this book, in its significance for later medieval thought, we can only point to the following characteristics.[1]

First, in logical sequence, he dispensed with inner illumination: again not in itself a new departure, and one in which he was preceded by the Aristotelians of the thirteenth century, especially St. Thomas Aquinas, together with whom Scotus adopted instead the doctrine of abstraction for knowledge of what is universal. But in Scotus's case that had two important consequences. The first was that it also dissociated the Franciscans, among whom illumination had found its main adherents in the middle and later thirteenth century, from the doctrine as well: for within a few years of his death, Duns's system became the official teaching of the order. Henceforth illumination ceased to be a formative influence upon subsequent thinking.

The second and more immediate consequence was upon Scotus's own thinking. Although, as we have just remarked, he accepted abstraction for knowledge of universals, its role was entirely different from that which it had in the full-bodied Aristotelian metaphysics of Thomism: for not only did Scotus uphold direct individual cognition by the intellect, but both universals and individuals were themselves subordinated to the ontological primacy of the common natures constituting all being. That together with the notion of univocity and the formal distinction, at once to transcend and explain their presence in all knowledge and existence, was Scotus's distinctiveness as a philosopher. From that standpoint universality and singularity are merely aspects of the same nature, of itself indifferent to either. But whereas in its actual existence it is individual, as a universal it can only be known in the intellect; indeed, strictly speaking a common nature is not universal at all, but merely common in a generic not a numerical sense. This was Avicenna's meaning, taken over by Duns Scotus and in due course opposed by Ockham, when he said that equinity, as the nature of horse, is only equinity, neither singular nor universal. An individual horse or a universal concept of a horse in the mind—as an intelligible species—is only

1. For much of what follows see: A. B. Wolter, *The Transcendentals and Their Function in the Metaphysics of Duns Scotus* (Washington, 1946); S. Day, *Intuitive Cognition: A Key to the Significance of the Later Scholastics* (New York, 1947); and *Duns Scotus: Selected Writings*, ed. A. B. Wolter (London, Edinburgh, 1962).

one or other of the two ways in which the same nature of horse can be encountered: it is individuated by what Duns called a contracting difference—or occasionally "thisness" *(haeceitas)*, a term given currency by his followers—which limits it to a numerical unity, where alone it is less than a numerical unity, i.e., does not exist as this or that individual; it owes its universality to abstraction by which again, as we have just said, it is not a numerical unity. According to which of these two ways it is known we have two different kinds of knowledge, each equally accessible to the intellect and having an essential order between them from individual to universal as different modes of the same reality. The reality therefore remains the same but the modes of conceiving it differ, namely as individual and universal.

Individual knowledge—of an individual horse or man or stone—is direct knowledge of existence, called by Scotus intuitive knowledge; it requires neither abstraction nor any mediating species or image but merely the direct presence of the object known to both the intellect and the senses, which know it concomitantly and immediately. Scotus thus joined the line of his immediate Franciscan predecessors and contemporaries in maintaining the Augustinian tradition of direct individual cognition by the intellect; but where thinkers such as Olivi and Vital du Four stopped short of conceding direct contact between the intellect and a material object, Scotus accepted it. He did so on the grounds that the intellect as a more perfect power can do whatever the senses as a less perfect power can do. But the senses can know individuals directly. Therefore the intellect can know individuals directly. Moreover, he went further and affirmed the possibility of immediate intuition by the intellect of individuals as individuals. Actually the possibility is not realized in man's present state through the effects of original sin. Consequently the intellect is confined to intuition of existence, not singularity, which taken in itself is the most perfect kind of knowledge. Hence knowledge of real existence is of an object's nature, namely the particular species *(species specialissima)* to which it belongs, as a horse is known in virtue of being a horse. That applies equally to the senses: their intuitive object is existence as existence. Neither intellect nor senses distinguish one individual from another save by what is incidental —their accidents—to them, such as the differences between Socrates and Plato as individuals: their size, and other physical and mental characteristics. Where there are no such individuating properties, as in, say, two white colors of equal intensity, there is no means of differentiating one from the other. Intuitive knowledge is thus always of individually existing natures and requires nothing more than their presence to be known to the intellect.

Abstractive knowledge on the other hand is, as we have said, of what does not actually exist but is known only as an intelligible species in the intellect. Such knowledge is only indirectly of individuals, reached by means of the active intellect within the soul abstracting the intelligible forms—of man, horse, and so on—from their sensory images derived from experience and stored in the imagination. Abstractive knowledge is therefore universal conceptual knowledge of the natures or essences abstracted from previous intuitive knowledge. Each is the work of the intellect and each bears upon the same natures, grasped in the one case individually in their existence and in the other universally in the intellect, which Duns calls a diminished likeness of the nature itself.

The interest of Duns's conception, then, is that in every case what is known, whether by the intellect or the senses, directly or indirectly, is a nature. There is not the dichotomy between individual and universal which there is in an Aristotelian epistemology and—paradoxically in view of the older accusation that Scotus put more emphasis upon the will's activity than the intellect's—the intellect is given a correspondingly more direct and active role, from the outset being involved equally in individual and universal knowledge. There is no precognitive stage that belongs to the senses as in the Aristotelian and Thomist doctrine of abstraction. The reason, as we have already said, is that nature or essence is primary as that which exists prior to its individual or universal determinations. Hence, again in contrast to St. Thomas's metaphysics, Scotus knows no distinction between an essence and its actuality as realized in existence. Essence is being, and not potential being that has to be made actual in order to exist. In that sense, again paradoxically in the light of the generally held belief about Duns's *a priori* universalism, he was prepared to take existence as he found it and not attribute it to modes which went beyond experience. The difference was that for Duns experience was as much conceptual as sensible. That was a function of his acceptance of individual intellectual cognition; there was no need to posit an ascending order of understanding from the individual given to the senses to the universal abstracted by the intellect from its images. The primacy of common natures guaranteed the reality of our concepts in immediately identifying the proper natures in things; abstraction was only a further stage in universalizing that knowledge already gained into its logical and conceptual forms with which proper—discursive —knowledge was concerned. Those concepts were thus merely the intelligible representations of the same natures known intuitively in their existence in individuals. For that reason there was no need to posit divine illumination, since it can add nothing to their certainty, as Duns replied to Henry of Ghent, to whom he stands in a similar relation to that in which Ockham was to stand to Duns, taking him as the sounding board for much of his own outlook. If, as Henry maintained, illumination overcomes the uncertainty of things, any certain knowledge it provides will not be of things themselves which must remain uncertain; if it is to overcome the uncertainty of our intellect, by the same token the intellect will no longer be the agent in what it knows; which Henry denies.

For Duns the problem of uncertainty was ontological not conceptual. It arose, that is to say, not from the absence of the essential natures in things, nor from our incapacity to grasp them—even if we could not go beyond them to their own essential singularity—but from the inherent contingency of all existence other than God's. Hence the problem of the reality of our concepts was distinct from the necessary certainty of what we know. The first could be explained metaphysically from the constituents of being; the second, logically by establishing the conditions for the truth value of propositions. Each is a further aspect of Duns's significance.

The first was directed to the problem, raised also by Henry of Ghent, of why there should be a discrepancy between our concepts of the nature of things and their physical nature, so that we see within them distinctions which do not exist physically. Henry's solution was to posit what he called a virtual distinction *(distinctio intentionis)* by which the object is able to produce different concepts of itself in the intellect having no physical counterpart. They therefore derive from the nature of the thing although they can only be perceived in the intellect. Duns's reply was that such a distinction failed to account for the reality of our concepts or the validity of essential prediction by which they are affirmed to belong intrinsically to something (as "rationality" is affirmed essentially of man). If a concept of difference is to be more than either a fiction or merely the same concept of the same thing, it can be of only some of the thing. That does not imply a physical distinction but rather a prior nonidentity within the thing, which enables the intellect to distinguish between them. Duns calls such a distinction a formal distinction within the thing itself *(distinctio formalis a parte rei)*. Unlike Henry of Ghent's virtual distinction, it is founded upon an ontological difference within things. Hence, what Henry saw as a discrepancy between concepts and things was for Duns resolved in the correspondence between concepts and the natures or formalities constituting things. That correspondence is expressed in the formal distinction, and comes as close as any system of thought in any epoch to a doctrine of a direct correlation between concepts and reality, where reality is conceived as whatever can be recognized independently by the mind, apart from any physical determinations it may have in individual existence.

In that sense the formal distinction enshrines the primacy of common natures. As specified by Duns the characteristics of a formality are that it is not a distinct thing but a quiddity or essence or nature, which as less than a numerical unity does not have its own distinct existence and hence is inseparable from the individual in which it exists as a numerical unity. It is thus distinct by nature but not as an individual thing. Which explains why it can be identified in the intellect while remaining indistinguishable physically; for it is only through the conjunction of a common nature with an individuating difference that an individual can exist at all, and a common nature can be contracted from an ultimate metaphysical abstraction into concrete being. In that condition they remain inseparable as there cannot be a man without his nature of a rational soul: not even God could separate one from the other, although he could annihilate a rational soul in its individual existence as a man.

The role of the formal distinction in Duns's system is protean: it embraces all finite—created—being as well as God's—infinite—being, and enables each to be subsumed under a common—universal—concept of being.

The omnipresence of formalities of varying degrees of perfection in every gradation of being is the foundation of Scotist metaphysics. It withdrew being, on the one hand, from the Aristotelian categories of potentiality and actuality, and, on the other, from the Platonic notion of independent forms or essences; and instead located all being in individual, or contracted, common natures which were the only mode of finite existence. That in effect represented the extension of Duns's theological explanation of the oneness of the Trinity, which originated with Gilbert de la Porrée (*ca.* 1076–1154), to all being. Just as there was a nonidentity between the divine persons that made them formally distinct while indissolubly the same nature, so with created beings, where, say, Socrates's humanity could be formally distinguished from Socrates and yet was inseparably and intrinsically the same as Socrates and did not exist apart from him. Duns thus brought to metaphysics the hypostasizing approach of Trinitarian theology, endowing each distinct figure with its own identity, from being as the most general of all concepts at one extreme to irreducible ultimate differences at the other. For Scotus the formal distinction guaranteed the reality of our concepts, however imperfectly, because it corresponded to the metaphysical realities within being itself. As conceived by him the notion of metaphysics was removed from its physical modes: movement, potentiality, act, the relation of matter to form, played no part in Duns's definitions of being, as they did for St. Thomas Aquinas. Compared with the latter's Aristotelian metaphysical categories, those of Duns must be called meta-metaphysics. Moreover, as for St. Thomas but in a radically different way, the justification for metaphysics was precisely that it transcended the physical world as a natural bridge to discourse of God. That was the supreme function of the notion of formalities. It provided the means for knowledge of God, not in himself: that was no more possible, naturally, than knowledge of individuals in themselves; but conceptually by recourse to transcendental concepts under which he could be subsumed in terms accessible to human understanding.

Now transcendentals were defined as those terms—being, one, true, good—which do not belong to any genus, regardless of what may belong to them. Of these the most universal is being as that which is presupposed in every other concept.

Until the time of Duns Scotus it was generally held that there was no single (univocal) concept of being that applied irrespectively to all being, because of the very diversity of being; and that so far as God is concerned, to conceive him as being is always by definition to conceive him as infinite being. Hence any concept of being applied to God is distinct from a concept of being applied to what is not God. At the very least they will be two separate concepts of being, related as infinite and finite. They will therefore be analogical—i.e., two distinct concepts related by some similarity between them—as opposed to univocal as one simple undifferentiated concept common to all that comes under it indifferently. Those were Henry of Ghent's grounds—in opposition to which Duns once again took his own point of departure—for denying that there could be a universal concept of being common equally to God and creatures; for even when God was called simply being, the term "being" is understood as infinite being; and so with all the other transcendentals applied to God. For that reason Henry had maintained that no univocal concept of being common to God and creatures was attainable: the concept which is of God, whether of being, truth, goodness, oneness, or any other, must always apply primarily to him and secondarily to creatures: in other words, it will have two meanings and so be two concepts. Henry, like the majority of the Augustinians, overcame the problem by the doctrine of illumination, so that special knowledge of God as supreme infinite being was gained in the intellect independently of knowledge of creatures. Duns, however, as we have seen, rejected that source. He also rejected the Aristotelian way of abstraction from sensible things; for they are by definition finite; and without experience of what is infinite there cannot, on Aristotelian principles, be a proper simple, i.e., immediate, concept of infinite being. If we had it, we should then know God really, which is not possible naturally. Hence any concepts we form of God on the basis of abstraction are merely composite, i.e., analogical, concepts derived from experience of creatures.

Duns accepted the arguments against the adequacy of an analogical concept of God; of itself it will never rise above knowledge of creatures, because direct knowledge of the second term of the comparison, namely, a simple immediate concept of God, is missing, and can be gained only indirectly by composing it from concepts taken from creatures, such as supreme being, or first cause or unmoved mover, which was the way of St. Thomas Aquinas in basing his proofs of God on analogous concepts of movement and causality. Duns did not, however, accept that univocal concepts of God were unattainable; if we could not abstract from differences, there could be no univocal concepts of anything. In fact, he held it is no less possible to form a concept of being freed from the modes of finite and infinite than it is to have a concept of finite being which prescinds from the categories of substance and accident; and by the same token with transcendental univocal concepts of all God's other perfections, wisdom, goodness, and so on. None of these is so immediately inseparable from infinite or finite that it cannot be conceived in abstraction from each. Of these only univocal being as the most universal of all concepts must extend to everything. It therefore comes first in the order of concepts of God and creatures. As univocal it is at once independent of all other concepts as the most absolutely simple of all and yet signifies what is real, namely that existence is possible, or, as Duns tends to express it, that being is not contradictory to something. For that reason Duns calls it a first intention, that is, a logical term that directly stands for a concept of something real, i.e., being, and not for another concept.

Duns therefore switched the order of procedure for knowledge of God from metaphysics to logic: that is to say, from a concept of God as actual being, when he must be defined as infinite being, to a concept of being as a logical term of first intention where its meaning is whatever may exist as opposed to what *does* exist in a particular mode. The shift epitomizes the ambivalence in Duns's outlook between the pulls of a pure metaphysics based upon the analysis of being as such, removed from its physical modes, and a logical conception of truth that complements it, but, as here, is also subordinated to metaphysics. The result was that Duns, perhaps more consistently Aristotelian in his logic than any of his predecessors, also took further than any of them the Neoplatonist legacy bequeathed by Porphyry in his Introduction to Aristotle's *Categories* (the *Isagoge*) of making Aristotle's logic a logic of essences. The significance of this development is that it in turn formed the point of departure for Ockham's deessentializing of Aristotle's categories, restoring them to what he believed was their original status simply as terms freed from all association with the essences, natures, formalities in which Duns had clothed them. Here, as in his theology, Ockham can be regarded as the direct successor of Duns Scotus taking his categories, as Marx in a different way was to do with Hegel, and turning them upside down. Thus, as we shall see, Ockham accepted Duns's doctrine of univocity but denied that a univocal concept was other than a concept; so that the concept of being, far from signifying an immediate reality as a first intention, was a second intention, a concept of being as merely the most abstract concept of existence, as opposed to nonexistence, with no direct rapport with anything.

Accordingly with Duns univocal being joins the other formalities, in this case expressing—imperfectly without reference to its modes—whatever can be. Its exact ontological status is ambiguous, at once logical and metaphysical, and as such expresses the ambiguity inherent in Duns's essentialist logic as Ockham was so clearly to see. But as the most universal of all concepts, at the furthest degree of abstraction with nothing beyond it save the capacity to be, it is at once emptied of all other concepts and contained in all other concepts as their subject. That for Scotus meant that being is both the first object of actual distinct knowledge, since it cannot be resolved into further concepts and what he called the first adequate object of the intellect as that which it knows first and which extends to knowledge of everything else. Here again he departed from both his Augustinian predecessors, especially Henry of Ghent who made God first object through a special illumination, and the Aristotelians who sought it in the intelligible species abstracted from images of individual things. Only being, by the double primacy of commonness to concepts reducible to further concepts, like genus, species, and individual, and virtuality to concepts of ultimate (individual) difference—which are irreducible to further concepts but from which the concept of being can be derived—extends to knowledge of everything else. In that way Duns was able to overcome the need for inner illumination and the limitations of existential knowledge in arriving at a concept of God. As with the formal distinction the concept of an adequate object derived from theological presuppositions, and in this case could only follow from what is held on faith: namely, God's existence as a transcendental being. As we shall see, he was to be criticized again by Ockham for the notion of a first adequate object just because knowledge of one individual could not give actual knowledge of another not itself immediately known.

Finally, Duns employed the concept of being for his proofs of God's existence, where having begun from it as a universal concept, he then analyzed it analogically into its attributes, both those with which it is coordinate—the other transcendentals—and those which are disjunctive—infinite and finite, eminent and dependent, perfect and imperfect, actual and potential, prior and posterior—to establish the essential order of dependence among all things upon God as the most eminent being. In confining himself to what is essentially ordered metaphysically, by the three ways taken from Henry of Ghent of eminence, efficiency, and finality, Duns was able to exclude the accidents that belong to the physical world. In place of Aristotle's and Aquinas's first mover as the first cause of everything else, Duns began from universal propositions concerning the nature of being, such as "All beings are ordered" or "Some effect can be caused." For only thus can the metaphysician arrive at a notion of a first being who confers being, as opposed to a first mover who merely moves. And to know God as first being is to know him more perfectly than to know him as first mover. There is no need to posit physical modes of existence, such as those of potentiality and act to reach the difference between infinite and finite being. They can be conceived metaphysically from the "law of disjunctives," that when being is divided into two extremes (potential and actual), if the imperfect is found among creatures, the perfect is in God.

Duns was thus able to make knowledge of God's existence independent of physical modes as he was able to make universal concepts common to God and creatures independent of metaphysical modes. In each case he operated with the notion of being as a capacity to exist—either in a particular way defined in relation to other ways or without any determination at all. His conception of being, as indeed of the other transcendentals and ultimate differences, thus stood at the confluence of logic and metaphysics: it was a term of first intention and belonged to an essential definition of the nature of something, in the Aristotelian sense; but while it lacked the Aristotelian actuality of concrete existence, it nevertheless had immediate ontological import—as something as opposed to nothing. In withdrawing both certain knowledge of being and knowledge of God from actual existence, Duns moved towards a new conception of truth as logical rather than existential, which Ockham was to take to its, literally, logical conclusion, of dispensing with any independent metaphysical foundation for our concepts—beyond existing individuals—at all.

That brings us to the other aspect of Duns's notion of certainty, in the conditions for the truth value of propositions. It can be regarded as a pendant to his view of being, just discussed, and represents a logical development of the first importance among his immediate successors, beginning with Ockham. It arose, as we have said, from the absence of the certainty which came either through divine illumination or the superior reality accorded to universals abstracted in the Aristotelian and Thomist manner from sensible individuals. As with Ockham after him, Scotus owed his concern to overcome the limits of existential knowledge to his Christian awareness of the contingency of all created existence. Here as elsewhere he initiated what Ockham was to pursue more rigorously, in the process criticizing Duns's arguments while accepting his assumptions. Thus, where, as we shall see, Ockham restricted necessary knowledge to what could only be known in self-evident propositions or could be shown to follow necessarily from them in strict demonstrations, Duns enumerated four kinds of knowledge that he classed as necessarily certain: self-evident propositions, in which knowledge of the meaning of the terms brings immediate and necessary assent to their truth; things known through experience, inductively; our own actions; and things known in the present by the senses. The first and third need the senses merely as their occasion: they would still be true even if the senses erred. The second and fourth can be made necessary syllogistically through a middle term based upon the principle of causality: that whatever occurs by means of a natural agent, which is not free, has that agent as its necessary cause. By Ockham's standards these four ways taken as a whole were inadequate; but together with his concept of being and the other transcendentals, and his proofs for God by means of the notion of what can be caused, Duns pointed towards a conception of certainty derived from the logical relation of terms and propositions, above all self-evident, i.e., analytic, propositions, from which, when the terms are known, there cannot be dissent: it was in that sense that he sought to re-interpret St. Augustine's doctrine of illumination, where the eternal forms, in the light of which Augustine said the mind perceives truth, are the first principles that it grasps immediately.

Despite the contentiousness of areas of Scotus's epistemology and metaphysics, its main import was away from their dependence upon actual modes of physical existence and to a greater reliance upon the independence of our concepts and the internal consistency of the terms and propositions formed from them. For all its philosophical subtlety his is essentially the work of a theologian seeking a metaphysical basis for a natural theology, as Duns himself expressly declared in taking the side of Avicenna against Averroës, that knowledge of God belonged to metaphysics, not to physics. The very restriction which metaphysics imposed, by excluding that which could only be known through the senses, limited the natural truths about God: for the metaphysician he was *par excellence* infinite being; but his omnipotence was a matter of revealed truth which could only be believed.

That leads us to the final aspect of Duns's significance, the theological conclusions he drew from God's omnipotence, especially as they concern the order of grace and free will.[2]

It used to be commonly held that in some way Duns was a voluntarist in theology and ethics, giving primacy to God's will in his decrees and to man's in his actions. If it is true of Duns, certainly, so far as God is concerned, it is equally true of every other Christian thinker. Indeed what is striking about the Scotist explanation of God as creator is the elaboration of a divine psychology in which God first (logically, not temporally) knows himself, then the ideas of all possible things which he produces, initially as intelligible objects in his intellect, and subsequently as creatures outside himself through his will. There is a similar logical sequence in the generation of the divine persons in God. Ockham was once again to reject out of hand any such series of logical instants in God as incompatible with his indivisibility. Yet their very speculative extravagance shows how far Scotus was from identifying God's actions with his will in any unqualified sense of merely willing, without also knowing what he wills.

Similarly in relation to his creatures, the arbitrariness of God's will is simply the unconstrained freedom of an omnipotent being to decree whatever does not lead him to contradict himself. That, as we have said, was nothing new; nor did Scotus again, from the standpoint of God's nature, ever consider the will in isolation from his other perfections. Whatever God does or can do is by definition good since as supreme being he is also supreme good. He therefore wills for the best as he always wills knowing what is the best.

It is when we change the perspective and consider God's omnipotence in relation to what he has already willed, in the order he has created, that his omnipotence is displayed; for he could change whatever he has decreed and either do directly what he normally does through created agents or do differently or not do it at all, just as he could have created a different world

2. For Scotus's conception of grace and merit see W. Dettloff, *Die Lehre von der Acceptatio Divina bei Johannes Duns Scotus* (Werl/Westf., 1954).

or no world or a better world than the one he has created. In pointing to the contrast between what God has decreed by his ordained power and what he could do by his absolute power, Scotus focused, as we mentioned in the previous chapter, upon its application to the dispensability of created grace and charity—the terms for Scotus are interchangeable—in meriting eternal life. Here the operative term is God's acceptance: it is the end which the infusion of a habit, or state, of grace into an individual soul serves, inclining its subject to acts of merit and resistance to sin beyond his own natural powers. Acceptance by God of someone for eternal life therefore comes before grace: in Scotus's words, "A person is accepted before grace is conferred." While by God's present dispensation the human will and charity work together in performing a meritorious act, which God recompenses with eternal life, by his absolute power he can reward the will directly and accept someone for eternal life without preceding charity. The reason once again is that God can do directly what he ordinarily does through second causes to realize his purposes, in this case the sanctification of an individual soul: grace is merely the secondary agent in its attainment, dependent upon a prior act of free will as the principal agent. The latter is accordingly independent of any habit; otherwise it would not be free. The role of grace and charity is thus not to move the will or to facilitate its capacity to act, but to give its acts a perfection and intensity that the will cannot bring to them naturally.

It is their very ontological independence that enables God to accept an act of will independently of any habit of grace where ordinarily he does so from their concurrence in the same act. No contradiction is involved just because the will can act alone. God simply confers the same gratuitous gift of eternal life by gratuitously willing to do so directly instead of through an equally gratuitous gift of preceding grace. He thereby achieves the same end by different means. Nor does his—absolute—power to bypass grace imply any derogation from its intrinsic goodness. Indeed, since grace of its very nature inclines to good and contradicts sin, if the will's actions were dependent upon it, they would necessarily be good. Which is the reason why grace cannot be the principal, and so indispensable, cause in a meritorious act; for Scotus, in common with scholastic tradition, but more insistently than many of his predecessors, makes a freely elicited act of will the source of all good and bad—as opposed to morally indifferent—acts. Free will is therefore inseparable from merit and sin alike, although, as we shall mention again shortly, it is by reference to God's decrees that they are such. The act, then, whatever its nature, must always be from the will and its acceptance—or rejection—from God: they are the constants. In the case of his acceptance the issue is whether God acts directly or through the mediation of grace; in either event it is his decision which renders an act meritorious and worthy of eternal life. How he does so, therefore, has nothing to do with the will's own power to transcend its natural limitations or to prompt or compel God's reward—the heresy of Pelagius. It involves only God's freedom to choose how his will should be done, the opposite of Pelagianism, in holding that God is not necessitated by anything created. He is thus no more obliged to accept an act because it is informed by grace than to accept an act without any supernatural form. And whichever he does he will do so equally freely and ordinately.

In thus exemplifying God's freedom to do whatever is logically possible, i.e., noncontradictory, Duns inaugurated a theological development that continued in an unbroken line to Luther.[3] Its adherents went beyond any group or school; they were drawn from Scotus's own pupils or early followers, like John of Bassoles, Antonius Andreas, Francis of Meyronnes; Franciscans of widely varying affiliations, like Alexander of Alexandria, William of Nottingham, Francis of Marchia, Robert Cowton, William of Rubione, John of Reading; thinkers of no fixed allegiance, like Henry of Harclay, John Baconthorpe, and, as already mentioned, Durandus of St. Pourçain; Ockham and his followers, such as Robert Holcot, Adam Woodham, John of Mirecourt, Thomas of Buckingham; Gregory of Rimini the most thoroughgoing Augustinian theologian and, with Thomas Bradwardine, arch anti-Pelagian of the fourteenth century; John of Ripa and subsequent thinkers like Henry of Hesse and Peter d'Ailly, continuing through the fifteenth century to Gabriel Biel and ultimately Luther. I have purposely cited so many names as witnesses to the diversity of standpoints associated

---

3. The account of the following thinkers is based principally upon W. Dettloff, *Die Entwicklung der Akzeptations—und Verdienstlehre von Duns Scotus bis Luther* (Munster/ Westf., 1963) as a sequel to his earlier book on Scotus, *Die Lehre von der Acceptatio Divina bei Johannes Duns Scotus.* It seems to me to establish irrefutably the Scotist lineage of the discussion over supernatural habits, and thereby to dispose of the claim that it is peculiarly Ockhamist or Nominalist.

with Scotus's doctrine of created grace. It is therefore irrational to treat a notion, which originated with a "Realist" and was upheld by many other "Realists," as the hallmark of a "Nominalist" theology. The current assumption that it is Nominalist is nevertheless in danger of becoming the new orthodoxy about later medieval theology; it can only lead to tangling together what must be kept disentangled.

The widespread belief that God could dispense with created habits is Christian before it is anything else; it represents a theocentric awareness of God's freedom, which, as already mentioned, is one of the dominant intellectual motifs of the later Middle Ages. As such, it was the common property of diverse philosophical and theological standpoints, presupposing only a common acceptance of the first article of the Creed, of belief in an omnipotent God. That diversity is expressed in the different applications given to God's freedom over created grace. Scotus did not go beyond stating it in terms of God's freedom from dependence upon created forms for the order he had ordained; nor on the whole did Ockham, although as we shall mention he gave a much wider application to God's absolute power and elaborated the argument for it over grace and acceptance. Gregory of Rimini, on the other hand, from an extreme anti-Pelagian view of man's natural—post lapsarian—disabilities which, in contrast to the optimism of Scotus and Ockham, allowed human actions no moral self-sufficiency or freedom from sin, made a complete separation between uncreated grace as God's own acceptance and created grace as the gift of the Holy Spirit. God could annihilate the latter entirely and yet still confer blessedness. John of Ripa showed something of the same approach. Others, notably Francis of Meyronnes, an early Scotist, and Robert Holcot and Adam of Woodham, a Dominican and Franciscan, respectively, and both Ockhamists, came nearer to what has been called negative speculation in stressing God's freedom to the point of arbitrariness. Thus, according to Meyronnes, God could damn someone who loved him and reward someone who hated him. To Holcot also there was no necessary correlation between grace and God's love, so that someone loving God less could be loved by God more than someone else, as in fact was the case with someone damned living in present grace and someone blessed existing in mortal sin. Correspondingly, God himself could deceive or mislead a man, making him believe what was not true and rewarding him for his belief. He would then be rewarded for his faith, which is independent of its truth or falsity. Adam of Woodham reaches a similar conclusion, but in the different context of God's revelation of the future which as still to come is contingent and so need not occur. Revelation could therefore be falsified. In addition, Adam also held that since there is no immutable order between grace and acceptance, or between sin and damnation, which God could not supersede, he could reveal to someone at present in charity his future reprobation.

These flights of paradox should not be misplaced. Although they introduced an ethical relativism and indeterminacy that could not fail to derogate from the intrinsic goodness of grace and its inherent necessity in the economy of salvation, their principal role was to illustrate God's freedom from an invariable order of second causes. No created act or habit of itself counted toward God's acceptance because there was no proportion between them. Blessedness was entirely from God's bounty. In that sense it was less man's than God's freedom from grace that was the main consideration. That is why, despite the periodic accusations of Pelagianism leveled against them, the upholders of this standpoint could confidently claim that theirs was the opposite of Pelagius's in making all reward depend upon God's freely conferring it and not upon free will's eliciting it.

It is arguable that Duns's doctrine of ethics was his most potent legacy to the later Middle Ages. For in making God's will the sole arbiter of good and bad by reference only to what he wills, Duns effectively subsumed ethics under logic and began the slide to ethical relativism: something is good because God as good wills it rather than it is willed by him because it is good; and since he can will whatever is not self-contradictory, the only thing that God cannot will is hate of himself as the highest good. Love of God above all other things is the supreme and immutable imperative and with it the obligation to love what God loves and hate what he hates. That is the foundation of all ethics and merit. By his ordained power it is expressed in his commandments. But just because God is both infinitely good and infinitely free he could have decreed other precepts no less good and equally binding: he could have permitted murder, as he did when he commanded Abraham to sacrifice his son Jacob; or not have enjoined private property so that there would have been no such offense as theft to prohibit; and similarly he could have continued to allow polygamy to be practiced as it had been among the Old Testament patriarchs. Each of these is possible because none involves God in any contradiction.

Paradoxically, this relativism comes from God's absoluteness as infinitely good and infinitely free. In thus allying them Duns opened a gap between the actual and the possible whose tension was one of the main elements governing later medieval thought. It had its counterpart in nature where God could separate matter and form through his power to create directly what he normally produces by a second cause; then the cause is not part of the effect.[4] That again was to be taken further by Ockham and his successors to whom God's power to separate or keep separate whatever is ontologically distinct but naturally coalesces—like form and matter—was a universal principle ever liable to be invoked. For them as for Duns these were each different facets of the same embracing contingency inherent in all creation. Duns, however, was content merely to posit it rather than pursue its implications. That was his difference from many others, like Francis of Meyronnes, in the succeeding generation. It also, as we have mentioned, led Scotus to a logical rather than an ontological conception of truth, which again became one of the hallmarks of the fourteenth century. In these different ways he began the reorientation in philosophy and theology which came after him.

That brings us to Ockham.[5] If he more than anyone was responsible for the subsequent change in outlook, it should perhaps be apparent from what has already been said that it consisted in more than the introduction of something called Nominalism. Ockham crystallized the tendencies we have been considering. The question of sources and pedigrees applied to him is even less germane than it is to Scotus: it is a matter not of others' influence upon him but of his reactions against others. That, as we have suggested before, is the case above all in his attitude toward Duns Scotus. Ockham's relation to Scotus is dialectical in the strict sense of his having resolved many of his own concepts in opposition to Scotus's.

That opposition varies from outright disagreement over first principles

4. Duns Scotus, *Opus Oxoniense*, II distinction 12, question 2.

5. This discussion is based upon my *William of Ockham: The Metamorphosis of Scholastic Discourse* (Manchester, 1975). See also S. Day, *Intuitive Cognition;* P. Boehner, *Collected Articles on Ockham* (New York, 1958); *William of Ockham: Selected Writings*, ed. P. Boehner (London, 1957). L. Baudry, *Guillaume d'Ockham: sa vie, ses oeuvres, ses idées* (Paris, 1950); E. A. Moody, *The Logic of William of Ockham* (reprint ed., New York, 1965).

to different interpretations or modifications of the same principles. To draw up a balance sheet will not convey that relationship. For all their divergencies, Ockham's outlook as he formulated it would be inconceivable without Scotus; it was largely framed in response to Scotus's. That is as true for those concepts central to Scotus's thinking which Ockham rejected—the formal distinction in all created beings as well as in God; the notion of a common nature and contracting difference in everything; intelligible species in knowledge of essences; the primacy of being as first adequate object of the intellect and first distinct object of knowledge; virtual knowledge of one thing through another; the psychology of logical instants in God—as of those he accepted or modified: intuitive and abstractive knowledge, as well as interior and past knowledge in the memory; a logical conception of truth in the need to overcome the contingency of existential knowledge; the rejection of illumination; the denial of a real distinction between essence and existence; the same overriding awareness and a much wider application of God's absolute power in grace and nature and its extension to knowledge; the univocity of being and the other transcendentals applied to God and creatures, leading Ockham to an outright denial of analogy at all; a formal distinction between the divine essence and persons; a persuasion for God's existence salvaged largely from criticism of Duns's elaborate proofs; the practical nature of theology; a similar conception of ethics and explanation of the eucharist in the transubstantiation of the bread and wine.

These are merely the more palpable expressions of the interdependence of Ockham's and Scotus's ideas, like the configurations produced by a subterranean stream continually at work. Thus to take some of the more egregious examples, the Prologue to Ockham's Commentary on the *Sentences,* his most comprehensive though not most synthetic work, on the nature of theology and its relation to evidential knowledge is largely conceived as a discussion and critique of Scotus's positions; so are the greater part of the trinitarian and theological distinctions, or chapters, which constitute the main body of the first, and, in Ockham's case, the longest and most complete, book; the prolonged treatment of relation as a category in books one and two and in the free—quodlibetal—questions; the moral and theological virtues in the main part of book three and again in the quodlibetal questions; causality in book three and the quodlibetal questions;

evidence for God as creator in book two; God's attributes and infinity in book one and the quodlibetal questions; love of God in book one; the relation of man's will to his intellect in book two; to say nothing of justification, predestination, God's foreknowledge, and divine ideas, for all of which Scotus's ideas were formative in the enunciation of Ockham's own. To seek, therefore, to claim Ockham as either the disciple—the recent tendency—or antagonist of Scotus is to misconceive the reciprocity of their relationship. It is one of outlook and counter-outlook within a shared recognition of the same problems. Between them they formulated the issues which were to be the dominant ones in knowledge and belief for the next century. Despite their radically opposite casts of thought they can thus be regarded as joint agents in the intellectual changes that ensued.

Within that common framework Ockham's point of departure was at the other extreme from Scotus in holding to the exclusively individual nature of all being. It is that which made their systems irreconcilable. Scotus, as we have seen, assumed a direct rapport between the mental and the real; with the formal distinction the hypostasizing of concepts reached its summation, giving every mental category and distinction its ontological counterpart as a quiddity or essence or nature or ultimate difference. To that extent Duns took further than anyone else the tendency to treat every concept and logical category as the expression of a metaphysical reality.

That was the very position that Ockham set himself above all to oppose for failing to distinguish between the conceptual and the real. It thereby destroyed the basis of knowledge and truth that consisted precisely in the conformity of what is known in the intellect with what exists independently of it. But since universals, essences, quiddities, formalities, and all the other abstractions can only be known conceptually, in the intellect and not outside it, to endow them with an independent reality is to make whatever can be conceived true. The distinction between concept and figment, true or false, then vanishes; for with nothing beyond our concepts and the propositions affirming or denying them, there is no means of verifying their truth or falsity.

This confusion of the mental with the real was to Ockham the source of the confusions and absurdities he saw in the thinking of his own time. They could only be overcome by recognizing the primacy of existence as the condition of any knowledge at all. Knowledge of existence alone constituted evident knowledge, which meant, since all existence was individual, that individual existence was the source of all proper knowledge. Ockham, if not the first to combine an individual epistemology with an individual ontology, was the first to apply the combination systematically to every branch of knowledge as well as to the meaning of theological truths. He did so not by denying any epistemological status to universals—the way of Nominalism—but by reducing the concepts, terms, and propositions comprising all logical discourse to their individual import, while at the same time accepting their universality as inseparable from all such discourse and necessary, i.e., demonstrative, knowledge.

The effect was to reverse the main direction taken by Christian thought since the time of St. Augustine, from which there had been only occasional departures, such as among the eleventh-century Nominalists. In contrast to his predecessors, including St. Thomas Aquinas and Duns Scotus, Ockham accepted the irreducible discrepancy between universal concepts as exclusive to the intellect, and the individuals alone existing outside it. Instead, therefore, of asking how the individual derives from a universal nature or essence, he sought to explain how in a universe of individuals the intellect comes to conceptions that are not individual. What had been an ontological problem, to be resolved by metaphysics, became with Ockham exclusively a psychological and logical matter, to be resolved conceptually —in how the mind forms concepts—and logically—over the way in which they are related to other concepts and things as terms and ordered in propositions. That was to substitute a conceptual and a logical order for a metaphysical order. It changed the basis of scholasticism, redirecting inquiry away from what was metaphysically conceivable—above all in providing a metaphysical explanation of universals in the way just exemplified by Duns Scotus—to what could be known and inferred from natural experience. That, as we have said, was to make knowledge of individual existence the source of all evident knowledge. For Ockham the operative terms in all discourse—epistemological, logical, theological, physical, political— were evidence and meaning, measured on the one hand by what could be known immediately from experience, and on the other by its relation to the concepts, terms, and propositions in which all knowledge is expressed. With him the preoccupation over what could be known, and with what degree of certainty, displaced the predominantly speculative interest of his predecessors; where they had employed concepts more as metaphysical bricks to build systems, he and his successors treated them for the knowledge and certainty they could yield. In that sense Ockham's analytical approach marked the ending of medieval system and with it the narrowing of the area of inquiry to what was accessible to experience and susceptible to analysis, logical, grammatical, mathematical, physical, and theological. Within essentially the same framework of a predominantly Aristotelian conception of knowledge and Christian belief, new modes of thought and interpretations of existing knowledge and belief were arising, marking, as we have said, a fundamental shift in outlook.

Beginning with evidence, we have already observed the recognition in different ways by both Scotus and Aureole of the inherent limitations upon knowledge of existence, and Duns's attempts to establish the ways in which certainty could be attained. Ockham systematized that recognition in making all knowledge in origin existential. From the outset the problem of evidence was at the center of his epistemology and logic, opening the Prologue to his Commentary on the *Sentences*. He defines it by means of Scotus's division of simple knowledge, i.e., of concepts, terms or things taken for themselves as opposed to knowing in them in propositions (complex knowledge), into intuitive and abstractive. Evident knowledge is whatever can be known to be true, directly or indirectly; it therefore presupposes intuitive knowledge, which for Ockham, as for Duns, is knowledge of existence. The difference between intuitive and abstractive knowledge is precisely between knowing something evidently as a fact and knowing it in the intellect as a concept or a term. Only the first mode can give actual knowledge, as in Ockham's example of the proposition "Socrates is white." To know that it is true requires intuitive knowledge of both Socrates and his whiteness in addition to knowing of them in a proposition. Merely to have—abstractive—concepts of each is not of itself evidence of either; hence abstractive knowledge alone will not produce knowledge of anything real beyond its own terms and concepts known in the intellect. For that reason Ockham took intuitive knowledge as the foundation of all other knowledge, abstractive, universal, contingent, necessary. It was the prerequisite of whatever could be known.

That is where he departed from Duns Scotus. For Scotus, as we have earlier indicated, intuitive and abstractive knowledge represented different aspects of the same nature: intuitive of its individual existence, the only way anything could exist independently; abstractive of its common nature by means of an intelligible species known only in the intellect. One was not dependent upon the other; and although intuitive knowledge in being of real existence was more perfect than abstractive knowledge, which was only of a diminished likeness stopping short of the individual, it still did not enable an individual to be known in its own singularity, the most perfect of all knowledge and unattainable to man in his present fallen state. Thus, although Duns admitted direct intellectual cognition of individuals, it was not of singularity itself but of existence which was at the same time individual. The duality between individual and essence remained, expressed in the two different modes of knowing, of which only abstractive knowledge, as nonexistential, could enter into conceptual discursive knowledge. Far then from intuitive knowledge providing the evident support for all subsequent, abstractive, knowledge, it stopped short at immediate awareness of existence, leading to nothing beyond existence.

For Ockham, by contrast, not only was intuitive knowledge the condition for abstractive knowledge, but they were both immediately of the same individual thing. Since only individuals are real there were no such things as common natures, or species by which to know them. As Scotus had dispensed with the Thomist conversion of species, so Ockham dispensed with the Scotist intelligible species. All simple cognition must be direct, whether intuitively of individuals or abstractively of their representations in the intellect; the latter can also be universals abstracted from individuals of the same nature; but their status is purely conceptual, as the mind's recognition of similarity among members of the same genus or species and not as the disengagement of some common essence or nature inhering in the individuals belonging to it. To the extent that it can be said to exist as a quality in the intellect, but not outside, a universal can be said to be known intuitively, but the *knowledge* that it gives is still abstractive since it does not bear upon real existence or nonexistence, the criterion of intuitive evidential knowledge. In Ockham's own words: Abstractive knowledge can be understood in two ways:

> by one it is in respect of something abstracted from many singulars: and thus abstractive knowledge is nothing else than knowledge of a universal, of which

more will be said later. And if a universal is a real quality existing in the intellect, as can probably be maintained, then it would have to be conceded that a universal can be seen intuitively, and that the same knowledge is intuitive and abstractive, taking abstractive in this sense. . . . By the other sense abstractive knowledge is taken for what abstracts from existence and nonexistence and the other contingent [i.e., existential] circumstances which concern a thing or are affirmed of it. Not that something is known by intuitive knowledge that is not known by abstractive knowledge, but the same thing is totally and in every identical aspect known by both kinds of knowledge. They are, however, distinguished in this manner: that intuitive knowledge of a thing is knowledge in virtue of which it can be known whether a thing is or is not, so that if it is, the intellect immediately judges it to be and knows its existence evidently, unless impeded by the imperfection of such knowledge.[6]

The distinction then for Ockham—contrary to Duns—is over how the same, individual, thing, the same in all respects, is known; not over what is known or in what aspect. It is the difference between evident and inevident knowledge, designed to answer the question "Why are some propositions judged to be evident and others inevident?" Intuitive knowledge is the means of judging, by enabling the intellect to distinguish the real from the mental. As such, it is the touchstone of truth and falsity.

Intuitive and abstractive knowledge have thus a radically different import for Ockham from that given to them by Duns Scotus. For Duns, the presence or absence of the object differentiated one from the other together with all the accompanying impedimenta of intelligible species, common natures, and diminished likenesses. Ockham sweeps away the latter as mere fictions, and qualifies the former: while it is true that, naturally, intuitive knowledge cannot be without the existence of an object as its efficient cause, supernaturally God could conserve the vision of something seen intuitively that is no longer existent or present. Such a vision would still be intuitive because it would be of what had been present or could be known immediately, even though no longer present, for example, in continuing to see the light from a star which is itself not there to be seen. Like all intuitive knowledge it could not be doubted. Accordingly, any distinction between intuitive and abstractive knowledge based upon the existence of what is

6. *Commentary on the Sentences:* Prologue, q. 1. in *Opera Theologica et Philosophica* (New York, 1967), 1: 30–31.

known becomes purely contingent, as Ockham replies to Scotus; for just as abstractive knowledge can naturally be of what no longer exists, so by God's absolute power could intuitive knowledge be. For that reason—in contradistinction to Duns—it is equally of existence and nonexistence. It is that which makes it different from abstractive knowledge, which as we have seen is indifferent to either. Naturally, however, nonexistence cannot be known intuitively but only by God's omnipotence.

Ockham's doctrine of intuitive knowledge of nonexistents was until recently taken to epitomize what was generally regarded as his skepticism, which to many was the solvent of the medieval outlook. Something of that attitude was expressed by the commission of theologians established by Pope John XXII at Avignon in 1324 to examine fifty-one propositions extracted from his writings for their dubious orthodoxy. They included his view of intuitive knowledge of nonexistents which was duly censured as false and dangerous. However rash or unsound it may appear from a strictly dogmatic position at first sight, to Ockham and those like Bernard of Arezzo, Peter d'Ailly, Adam of Woodham and others who followed him, in his opinion, the distinction he was making between what occurred naturally and what could occur by God's absolute power, whether applied to intuitive knowledge or created grace, was designed to exhibit what was essential to the nature of the thing in question: in the case of intuitive knowledge that it is evidential and only secondarily and contingently existential. To whatever it was applied the distinction epitomizes not Ockham's skepticism—or indeed fideism with which it is usually joined—but his awareness of the contrast between what holds *de facto* and what could be *de possibili*. If it was Duns Scotus who more than anyone introduced it in that form, Ockham gave it its general application and currency which, as we have said before, made it one of the hallmarks of fourteenth-century thought.

If invoking God's absolute power tended to become in the end a device for expressing extreme paradoxes, for Ockham it was a device for keeping God at the center of creation. The appeal to his omnipotence helped to liberate both being and knowledge from the prevalent misconceptions over their nature by reducing them to the individuals which were the constituents of both. In that sense Ockham's outlook was at the furthest extreme from a naturalistic self-sufficiency. Since the interdependence of everything was the result of God's free concausation, he could as freely detach what is ontologically extrinsic to something else even though naturally inseparable. That applies to knowledge as much as it does to form and matter or quality and substance or anything else which constitutes a distinct entity. Just as God could have created one without the other, so he could conserve one without the other. In that way what was intrinsic to something could be differentiated from its contingent circumstances in which it existed. Granted an essential nature at all, its only necessary accompaniment was the presence of a creator to conserve it: nothing else was needed because God could do directly what he had ordained to be done through secondary causes.

That was the logic of God's omnipotence. Its invocation became the equivalent of the principle of economy, applied to God: the theological counterpart of the so-called razor (which was not Ockham's invention at all) that hypotheses should not be multiplied unnecessarily. It was stated by Ockham as follows:

> God can do some things by his ordained power and some by his absolute power. This distinction is not to be taken to mean that there are really two powers in God, because God's power is the same in God as outside him, and is himself in every way. Nor should it be so understood that God can do some things ordinately and some absolutely and not ordinately, for God can do nothing inordinately. Rather, his power to do something is sometimes to be accepted according to the laws which he has ordained and instituted; and this way God is said to be able to act by his ordained power. Alternatively, his power means his ability to do all that does not include a contradiction, whether he has ordained that it should be done or not, because God can do many things that he wills not to do, according to the Master of the Sentences [Peter Lombard, author of the Four Books of *Sentences* c. 1160 which became the basic theological textbook of the thirteenth and fourteenth centuries], distinction 43; and this is called his power by his absolute power.[7]

For Ockham the application of God's absolute power lay principally in substituting a wholly divine for a partially divine concausation, representing God's direct intervention in events normally performed by creatures and conserved by him. But it could also mean positing quite different alterna-

7. *Quolibet* 6, 1.

tives, as in the creation of another or better world or several worlds, or infinite beings. In both aspects its purpose was the same one of freeing God and creation from the inexorability of secondary causes—the continuing legacy of 1277. Whatever the form it might take, as identical with God himself his absolute power could only be for the best of all possible worlds.

For that reason, applied to intuitive knowledge of nonexistents, God in conserving such knowledge, after its object is no longer present or has ceased to exist, is not deceiving the person who has it. He is merely separating the knowledge itself, as an apprehension or immediate awareness of existence, from a judgment about its existence, or, when stated in a proposition, its truth. Since naturally apprehension and judgment, as assent, dissent, or doubt over what is known, are for Ockham separate acts, although judgment always depends upon preceding apprehension, supernaturally God can conserve apprehension without judgment on the same principle already enunciated by both Ockham and Scotus that, in Ockham's words, "Every absolute (independently existing—for Ockham—individual) being which is distinct in place and subject from something else absolute can exist by divine power after the other absolute is destroyed." Conversely, on the same principle, there could be assent to the existence or nonexistence of a nonexistent without evident knowledge of either. No contradiction is involved because different—separable—kinds of knowledge are involved. Similarly God could cause an act of belief that something absent is present; that again would not be a contradiction; for such belief would not be evident knowledge, and so the person having it would not be knowing evidently the existence of something that does not exist. What God cannot do—because it would be contradictory—is to cause evident knowledge, i.e., an intuitive apprehension of existence, that something is present when it is absent; for evident knowledge by definition is of what is or is not: otherwise it would not be evident. That applies equally to evident knowledge of nonexistence, the cause of which is precisely intuitive knowledge that something does not exist, leading to a judgment of nonexistence. The difference is that such knowledge can only be supernatural, because naturally there is no intuitive knowledge without an object and what is not cannot be an object of knowledge. Only indirectly—and so not intuitively—can it be inferred, from the absence of knowledge of something, that that thing does not exist.

There are three main implications of Ockham's notion of intuitive knowledge of nonexistents. The first is that it was intended to exclude any possibility of God's power to delude or mislead by the very distinction on which it is based between apprehension and assent. The second was that for the same reason it was not designed to induce doubt about the certainty of intuitive knowledge; whatever was known intuitively was known evidently as it existed or did not exist. Hence intuitively we can never know that something absolute that is apprehended does not exist; only that it is absent when conserved by God supernaturally. That is the difference between knowing intuitively a nonexistent, to which Ockham confines intuitive knowledge, and nonexistence, which is excluded from his discussion. By intuitive knowledge the certainty of what is known is assured. Third, however, on Ockham's account there is no means of distinguishing between psychological certainty—as in a false belief that something exists— and epistemological certainty. That is where his doctrine is inadequate. It also, in allowing that God could induce such an illusion (as a belief, not knowledge), lays itself open to the very charge that the distinction between apprehension and assent was designed to exclude: namely, that God could mislead the intellect into taking as true what was false. At the strictly epistemological level of not *knowing* as true what is really false, Ockham succeeds, but not at the psychological level of being misled into error, by believing that something exists which does not exist. Theologically and logically he had justification: the lack of absolute certainty in everything created is the pendant to belief in an omnipotent God; and evidence can be of what is not as well as of what is. But that very justification must also weaken the force of natural certainty.

Ockham was not the first to argue that God could directly cause intuitive knowledge without an object: Harvey of Natalis and John of Bassoles, one of Scotus's pupils, had already done so. But after Ockham it became a common view, held among thinkers as diverse and often opposed as John Buridan, Gregory of Rimini, and Peter d'Ailly. D'Ailly followed John of Mirecourt in distinguishing between absolute evidence, by which nothing can be known certainly, and conditional evidence where with God's concurrence something external can be known with sufficient certainty to be accepted as evidence. Gregory of Rimini on the other hand restricted supernaturally conserved intuitive knowledge to what could be known to exist, denying it to judgments of nonexistence. He also denied, as Ockham did, that God could deceive, contrary to Richard Fitzralph, Robert Holcot, John of Mirecourt (who nevertheless both denied intuitive knowledge of nonexistents), and Adam of Woodham, all of whom affirmed that in relation to the future God could mislead or cause Christ to be misled or to mislead over his prophecies; while Nicholas of Autrecourt, as we have seen, denied certainty to anything other than the principle of contradiction, which for Buridan, too, but without the extreme consequences drawn by Autrecourt, constituted absolute evidence.

The problem of evidence thus became one of the focuses of fourteenth-century philosophy and theology. For virtually every thinker concerned, including Nicholas of Autrecourt, it arose within a Christian context of a contingent universe created by an omnipotent God, where experience of existence must be the foundation of evident knowledge. Ockham crystallized it in that form by allying intuitive knowledge with God's omnipotence. Far from being an aberration on his part or that of his successors, it largely underlay the changed conception of knowledge which accompanied the doctrine of intuitive knowledge. That can be seen in the effect upon the nature of logic whose rules govern all knowledge and discourse.

In the first place, with intuitive knowledge alone evidential, and abstractive, its conceptual, nonevident counterpart, whatever cannot be reduced to intuitive knowledge in standing directly for real things of which its terms are verifiable, as in the example of Socrates and whiteness, cannot give evident knowledge. Accordingly, intuitive knowledge of one thing does not suffice for intuitive knowledge of something else. One thing can, as we shall mention shortly, be inferred from another thing but it can only be known actually if it is itself first known intuitively. That was to cut at the root of the entire Scotist notion of the concept of being as first adequate object of the intellect, contained in knowledge of everything else; and with it the formal distinction, both for the same reason that only that which could be known immediately in its real existence could be taken as real. But only an individual thing is real; hence it always comes first in the order of knowing, and the knowledge it gives can only be of real individuals whether they exist separately or in a real relation to one another. There are no halfway houses of virtual or formal distinctions: either something is the same or it is different. The only real distinction Ockham recognized within things was that between a substance and a quality as physical components constituting the same thing, as heat is the quality inhering in a hot substance, or whiteness in something white, or form in matter as the irreducible constituents of all physical being. That was the furthest Ockham could go in denuding an Aristotelian metaphysics of all nonphysical elements, by translating them into physical terms without overthrowing the received conception of the physical world: a step that Ockham was neither in a position, nor showed any indication of wishing, to take. For him it sufficed to give an individual import to all Aristotle's categories whether logical or physical. Beyond individual substances and qualities as physical entities he recognized no other existence. Hence, all real meaning had to signify one or other, either subsisting independently as substances, or inhering in substances as qualities.

The dissolution of all common natures and universal essences ontologically entailed a redefinition logically of the terms representing them. If there was only one kind of being—individual being—it followed that the diversity hitherto attributed to being, in the manner of Duns Scotus, belonged not to being but to the terms describing the same—individual—being. It was there that Ockham's greatest impact was felt. Formally he was not a logical innovator; beyond adopting the terminist category of supposition, introduced by the logicians of thirteenth century, notably William of Sherwood and Peter of Spain, Ockham's one departure from the traditional framework was his treatment of consequences or conditional propositions. It was in the exclusively individual import that he gave to all terms and propositions that he is distinguished from his predecessors. What they had for the most part regarded as metaphysical categories he treated as logical—and in another context physical—categories; he did so not because he was a logician who reduced philosophy and theology to logic, as he has been in the past depicted, but because his logic and philosophy were founded upon an ontology of individual existence and an epistemology of individual cognition. It is that which made logic central to his outlook, for it was there that he systematically sought to resolve the discrepancies between the exclusively individual nature of being and the universality of all proper knowledge.

Central to that purpose was the distinction between the different kinds of terms and the different meanings they could have in propositions. The first turned on the distinction between absolute and connotative terms, the second, between signification and predication. An absolute term was one that had what Ockham called a real definition: that is to say, it directly stands for something real, seizing its essential nature without reference to anything extrinsic to it, as "man" can be defined as a rational animal or a substance composed of a body and a rational soul. Hence the word "man" or "animal" always immediately and completely stands for a real being as something which exists independently. A connotative term on the other hand has a nominal definition: it does not directly signify something real, as a real definition does, but is a description which can equally apply to something which does not exist as well as to something which does. In either case it is of what does not correspond immediately to a self-subsisting thing, as "white" is equivalent to the expression "something having whiteness" or "chimera" to "an animal composed of goat, lion and man." Similarly with all conjunctions, verbs, adverbs, and other parts of speech: they all have a meaning expressed in a nominal definition, but none directly signifies an independent thing. Consequently connotative terms signify one thing primarily and directly and consignify or connote something else secondarily and indirectly. Thus "white," defined as something having whiteness, directly signifies the thing which is white and consignifies indirectly the whiteness inhering in that thing. That holds for many concrete terms—those denoting an actual thing—and all relative terms, which in the broadest sense are also connotative in signifying one thing and consignifying something else which is distinct, as "father" or "master" consignifies "son" or "servant." Indeed, of Aristotle's ten categories, into which all being is divided, only substance and quality are absolute terms because they alone are real; all the rest, quantity, relation, place, time, movement, and the others, merely connote substance or quality under different aspects: quantity a substance's length or breadth or shape, time its duration in a particular place, and so on. The same distinction between absolute and connotative terms helps to resolve the difference between concrete and abstract terms. Grammatically a concrete term can be an adjective, such as "white," where an abstract term is always a noun such as "whiteness." Logically a concrete term is always what we encounter intuitively and immediately as actual, before analysis into its components as having a real definition when a substantive—man or animal—or a nominal definition when an adjective—white or hot. When concretes and abstracts are both absolute terms they are synonymous; they only differ when one or other is connotative in the way that white and whiteness differ.

The importance of this distinction is that it reduces all differences between concrete and abstract terms when they are absolute terms—of real things—to terminological differences. That enabled Ockham to cut the ground from under the majority of his predecessors and contemporaries who treated the division between concrete and abstract as an ontological one between a thing's essence and its existence—as Aquinas did—or as a formal distinction between an individual (concrete) and its common nature (abstract) in the manner of Scotus. Where they are synonymous they mean the same thing, and differ only in their grammatical forms; where they are not synonymous their meaning can only be identified by translating the connotative term into its nominal definition to establish its meaning, whether as a mere form of words having no real import, like "chimera," or connoting something real, as "white" does.

Ockham's analysis of the diverse combinations that absolute and connotative terms can have, as abstract or concrete, displays with the rest of his logic—above all in his masterwork *The Sum of Logic*—a sensitivity to the nuances of language which brought a new dimension to fourteenth-century philosophy. With an intricacy worthy of the subtlety of Duns Scotus he directed it to the opposite end of dehypostasizing our concepts and terms. He did so principally by means of the distinction between real and nominal definitions, which anticipated Russell's theory of descriptions by nearly six hundred years, and with greater linguistic acumen and more far-reaching consequences. It effectively brought down the metaphysical edifice which had been built upon Aristotelian logic. For the first time, a grammatical and logical explanation, based upon the different endings words could take and their meanings, was substituted for the attempt to find specific counterparts for them in the real world. Thus where Scotus followed Avicenna into explaining that equinity must be the nature of horse, which comes before either its individuality or its universality, Ockham treated it as nominal definition corresponding to nothing distinct from a horse, but merely stating that a horse is a horse in virtue of being a horse. What had been taken for a metaphysical problem—of the existence of a common nature—became a logical problem of defining an abstract term.

Their confusion was what Ockham called a fallacy of a figure of speech; it arose again and again from treating a connotative term standing immediately for nothing real which exists as such—and may not exist at all—for something real: it represented a failure to distinguish a word's meaning from its grammatical form, thereby investing all abstract terms with an independent reality. Ockham was the first to expose it by reversing the order and recognizing that the diversity among terms came from language and not from being—or God.

He achieved a comparable effect by his other major logical distinction between affirming one term of another in propositions and signifying something real. That again was to reject their almost universal identification, by which whenever something was predicated of something else, for example, a species of an individual, in the proposition "Man is a species," both man (as subject) and species (predicate) must stand for real things: in that way once again universals and abstract terms were invested with an independent reality, even though they could not exist independently. That assumption, that whenever something was affirmed of something else it represented something real belonging to its subject, had been enshrined in the Neoplatonizing of Aristotle's predicables—the universal terms of definition, genus, difference, accident—and categories, begun by the fifth century Neoplatonist Porphyry in his Introduction to Aristotle's *Categories (Isagoge)*, which had become the inseparable accompaniment to the study of Aristotle's logic. Apart from reclassifying Aristotle's four predicables, as the means of defining any being, into five to include species and property and omitting definition, Porphyry treated them less as the prerequisites of identifying the subject of discourse than as the natures or essences present in all individuals, of which the latter are the expression. In particular he made genus and species—which had not been among Aristotle's predicables—equivalent to the natures or essences of individuals, predicated necessarily of whatever belongs to them; on that interpretation, the species "man" connotes the humanity inhering in all individual men as opposed to individual men signified absolutely, i.e., directly, for themselves as real individuals and nothing else. Similarly with genus, while difference, property, and accident became the characteristics differentiating genera, species, and individuals. In every case they represented the real constituents, whether essential or incidental, defining individuals.

That was the first and decisive step in a long tradition culminating in the formal distinction. By it the signification of a universal term such as "man" could only be understood through a prior analysis of man's nature in the light of the predicables defining him. Predication therefore came before signification, which presupposed the presence of inherent universal qualities in what was signified.

Ockham's reply was to reverse the order and maintain the significative role of all predicables as well as categories: namely that they denoted real individuals, either directly by genus and species or indirectly and connotatively by the other three predicables. They therefore represented not inherent essences or qualities, but concepts formed to signify the nature of things, which, as the latter's signs, are not the same as what they signify. Thus in the proposition "Socrates is a man," "man," as the species, stands not for itself as a separate nature but for the individual being that Socrates is. Logically a universal term like "man" is distinguished precisely because it can stand for many individuals; epistemologically it is distinguished in giving only indeterminate knowledge, for the very reason that it can stand for any number of like individuals indifferently; ontologically it is distinguished as a concept, which is to say that it has no independent standing at all. Taken for itself as a term or concept it is singular like everything else. Universality is therefore a logical and epistemological attribute; it rests upon predicability, not inherence. It was a distinction Porphyry and his medieval successors largely ignored. He and they therefore turned a logical relation into a metaphysical relation, expressed in the so-called Tree of Porphyry, of a descending order from genus to accident, where each superior term was taken to express a more universal nature than that which came below it and to be included in the less universal—a doctrine transposed by Duns Scotus to the order of knowing, with being as the most universal of all concepts as at once the first distinct object of knowledge and included in knowledge of everything else as less universal. To Ockham, on the contrary, terms were related as more and less universal not because of any such ontological or epistemological connection but in virtue of their greater or lesser universality in signifying more or fewer individuals: superior and inferior were measures of their degree of predicability, not part of a hierarchy of natures or of knowing. That must be the criterion of all terms taken significatively.

Not all terms can, however, be taken significatively: that applies not only to the parts of speech, the so-called logical constants *(syncathegoremata)* —verbs, adverbs, prepositions, conjunctions—having no significative function in not standing for something else, but also to those—nouns, adjectives, and pronouns—which can be the subject or predicate of propositions *(cathegoremata)*. In their case the reason can be either that they never denote anything real, as "chimera" does not, or that they are employed nonsignificatively to stand for nothing other than themselves as concepts or words. The difference between a term used significatively and nonsignificatively is explained by the different modes of supposition by which its meaning in a proposition can be identified. Supposition thereby provided the safeguard against the very fallacies that derived from the Porphyrian tradition of treating universal concepts and terms significatively as standing for an independent order of reality.

The distinction was introduced and popularized by the thirteenth-century logicians William of Sherwood (d. between 1266 and 1271) and Peter of Spain (d. 1277), who as Pope John XXI had instructed Stephen Tempier, bishop of Paris, to act over the Latin Averroists. The term *suppositio* means the substitution of one term for another, in the way that the pronoun "this" can stand for an individual—Socrates—in the proposition "Socrates is an animal" or for the proposition itself—"This is true." By knowing what a term stands for, it is then possible to overcome terminological confusions such as that of the paradox of the liar: for if in the proposition "What I am saying is false," "false" is predicated simply of the subject taken for itself (i.e., "What I am saying"), it does not signify anything other than the statement as a form of words, when it is self-referring; alternatively it stands for something other than itself (i.e., what has been previously said). Neither involves any contradiction, and so no paradox.

As we have said, supposition was the one terminist device taken over by Ockham from the terminist logicians. Yet his so-called followers came to be known as the Terminists because of its widespread of application. By allying it to an individual ontology, in which only individuals could have real signification, Ockham gave supposition a new significance; it was the means at once of pointing to the absence of any necessary correspondence between words and things and of correcting their divergence by establishing the appropriate meaning which a term has. Supposition was therefore the condition of truth, which depended upon the correct use of terms in propositions affirming or denying something.

As interpreted by Ockham a term can stand in a proposition in one of three different ways: significatively in personal supposition for some thing or sign other than itself; or nonsignificatively, either as a concept, in simple supposition, or as a word, in material supposition. The difference between them is not between standing for real things as opposed to concepts or words; it is between terms which signify, no matter what, and terms which stand only for themselves. For that reason supposition and signification are asymmetrical: all signification implies supposition, but not *vice versa*, because simple and material supposition are nonsignificative. That explains why it is possible to predicate one term of another without signifying either anything or anything real; for to say "Man is a species" can only refer to "man" as a concept (i.e., in simple supposition) since no such thing as species exists which could agree with man as something real when not understood as an individual being. On the other hand, in the proposition "Every man is an animal" "man" can be in personal supposition—significatively—because "man" stands for every individual man—as opposed to something common—who is also by definition an animal. Similarly with the propositions "Every spoken word is part of a sentence" or "Every species is a universal," where in each case the subject stands for something other than itself. On the other hand, in the proposition " 'Man' is a name," "man" can only refer to a word and so has material supposition, signifying nothing beyond itself as a conventional term, i.e., one that has its meaning imposed upon it in contrast to a natural sign, which a concept is. The elaborate rules Ockham enunciates, especially for personal supposition—which unlike the other two forms is the way in which a term is employed naturally, as opposed to a deliberate act on the part of the user—shows here as elsewhere his logical and terminological fertility; for all his demolition of received ideas his principal concern was the positive one of redefining knowledge and meaning in terms of an individual ontology.

That can be seen also in his theory of supposition itself where his departure from tradition consists precisely in denying independent signification to simple supposition—of concepts—because he denied universals any independent standing. He thus owed his interpretation not to terminist logic as such, but to his philosophical principles. For that he was opposed by other thinkers, who were not less traditional for adhering to the same logic, namely, Walter Burley, who wrote his treatise on *The Purity of the Art of Logic* expressly in reply to Ockham, and a younger contemporary, Walter Chatton, a Franciscan, who from the little yet known of his writings adhered to Scotism and was one of Ockham's most acute critics.

Supposition, then, was directed to the proper use of terms by distinguishing the sense in which they could be legitimately taken. It acted as the regulator in identifying the meaning that a term may have in a proposition and above all whether it can be verified in experience if it is supposed to represent something real other than itself. That made supposition of universal applicability. In itself it does nothing to terms; nor does it make someone an Ockhamist: it merely takes the terms in propositions and asks what they represent when they are related as subject and predicate. The great innovation that came with supposition, and Ockham's employment of it was the distinction between terms used significatively and nonsignificatively; in Ockham's case, harnessed to his distinction between absolute and connotative terms, it became the instrument in reducing to logical and conceptual status terms, above all universal and abstract terms like "being" and "essence," which had come to be treated as independent realities. Supposition enabled him to show that they signified either individuals or nothing beyond themselves as terms. The effect upon the metaphysical presuppositions of the time could not fail to be profound.

That brings us to knowledge in the proper sense of that which can be known and assented to in propositions, and with it to the role of universals. So far we have been concerned with Ockham's reasons why universals cannot be taken for reality in themselves and how their only significative function must be of individuals in the way that "man" as a species signifies many individual men. The question now is how such a universal term does so and what knowledge it can yield. As we saw when discussing abstractive knowledge, one of its meanings is something abstracted from many singulars as a universal. Hence for Ockham, as for the majority of medieval thinkers, universals were the result of abstraction by the intellect of what was common to individuals of the same nature. Now it was precisely over that nature that Ockham diverged from his predecessors. For Aquinas and, as we have seen, in a different way, Duns Scotus, that which was abstracted was the essence or form or nature, freed from its material accompaniments, and which inhered in like individuals as the source of their likeness. For Ockham, on the other hand, it was merely a likeness among similar individuals which the mind recognized in members of the same genus or species: it did not stand for any quality or nature distinct from the individuals themselves.

Ockham distinguished three degress of similarity. The most perfect is that of species in its most specific sense (as a *species specialissima*) immediately beyond which come individuals, as "man" is the *species specialissima* of individual men. As last in the order of universal terms it has the greatest real identity so that although its members do not constitute a single whole —because their common similarity is only a mental abstraction—were they able to do so, such a whole would be identical with its parts. Next comes genus, which has only imperfect similarity with its individual members, since they are not of the same nature: in Ockham's words "neither entirely similar nor entirely dissimilar, but similar in some respects and dissimilar in others," as man and ass belong to the same genus of "animal," or man and angel meet in the same univocal concept of "substance," or black and white having the same community of "color." Both genus and species, however, in being abstracted from real determinate individuals can be taken concretely as immediately standing for individuals absolutely, as opposed to connotatively. In contrast, the third and most imperfect degree of similarity has no such ontological community, but is merely a conceptual similarity based upon a univocal concept of being—or any other concept —in the manner of Duns Scotus. As such it is the one means of uniting under the same concept both God and creatures without existential reference to either, since there is no conceivable similarity between them, either essential or accidental. Those of whom it is affirmed thus have nothing real in common. Hence, ontologically, beyond the level of abstraction represented by genus, real similarity ceases; any further similarity is solely of concepts.

It was on the basis of generic and specific similarity that all universal knowledge, namely, that which is contained in universal propositions, which for Ockham in the Aristotelian tradition was the only proper knowledge, proceeded and indeed was made possible. For only if a term could be affirmed of all the individuals coming under it, as a genus or a species —the two main kinds of similarity—could there be valid deduction from premises to a conclusion, the foundation of all strict, or scientific, knowledge. Paradoxically, then, the havoc Ockham wrought with his predecessors' interpretation of universals, in freeing them of any independent metaphysical standing, served to reaffirm their role in all inferential and demonstrative knowledge. By giving genus and species an exclusively individual import he was able to explain the relation between individuals. Far from Ockham's being a world of discrete individuals having no connection with one another, its intelligibility derived precisely from their similarity and their dependence upon one another as cause and effect.

Within the limits of natural certainty governing the created order Ockham totally accepted the regularities of being, upon which all knowledge rested, as he did also of moral norms. It is not too much to say that, in his outlook, similarity and causality are the pivots of all order and intelligibility. Nothing could therefore be more misconceived than the older widespread belief that he denied either universality or causality. What he did was to treat them empirically as deriving from experience of individual being, as we have just seen in the case of similarity.

So far as causality was concerned, on the principle that intuitive knowledge of one thing does not give intuitive knowledge of another, a cause cannot be inferred from its effect, just because naturally each must be known intuitively, and because supernaturally whatever is an absolute—as a real substance or quality—could by God's absolute power be conserved separately from any other absolute with which it always naturally exists or operates in conjunction. But given experience of two things or events, so that whenever there is one the other always follows, and without the first the second does not occur, it can then be inferred that the first is the cause of the second. Moreover, having established inductively that their relation holds for all members of the same species—in Ockham's example, that a certain herb cures a particular ailment—on the universally necessary principle that causes of the same species always produce effects of the same species, it can then form the basis of an inductive, or *a posteriori*, demonstration, that is, one beginning from the effect and leading to the cause. That applies principally to efficient cause but it holds also for the other causes, although final cause when it is an intention or end in the mind of an agent cannot be manifested physically. Whatever the kind of cause, however, cause and effect constitute a real relation between two terms.

Hence relation is not, contrary to another of the misconceptions about Ockham, merely the work of the intellect, as a purely mental construct: it represents an actual connection between things. What it is not is some third thing distinct from the two things or terms which are related. Like all the categories, other than substance and quality, relation is a connotative term describing substances or qualities, in this case as similar as two white things are or as cause and effect. To that it need only be added that the entire relation of God to creatures is that of first cause to second cause; so that God's presence in everything as concause and conserving cause, as the condition of the existence and the continuance of second causes, provides the main justification for his power to suspend the normal order between second causes in nature and grace. Reliance upon causality is therefore at the center of Ockham's outlook—and his unorthodoxy.

As it affects knowledge, causality operates through similarity, exemplified in the universal principle just stated that causes of the same species always produce effects of the same species. That as we have just seen is because similarity is the source of universality, upon which all proper knowledge depends. Only if a universal term can be affirmed univocally of another as its subject can one proposition be inferred logically from another. As we considered with Duns Scotus, a univocal term is one that stands for a single common concept, as opposed to an equivocal term which can be of two or more terms—as "dog" is the same word for an animal and a star and a portrait of a dog. For that reason only a univocal term can enter into universal discourse because it is unambiguous and therefore can alone be affirmed essentially of whatever its concept stands for, as the term "man" represents a concept standing for all individual men. Although strictly a univocal term, namely, of genus or species, can only be affirmed absolutely of a subject, as "animal" of "man" or "man" of "Socrates," so that it signifies it immediately and individually without reference to anything else intrinsic or extrinsic, in its broad sense a univocal term can also be used connotatively to signify either a part or property of a subject or something additional to it, as "rational" can be affirmed of "man." In either case, if the predicate—as a predicable—is more general than the subject and signifies what is essential to it, it represents an essential definition in what was called the first essential mode. If, on the other hand, the subject is included in the definition of the predicate defining it, as "able to laugh" affirmed of man is an attribute of man, or "creature" affirmed of God includes God as creator, then it is by the second essential mode. Together they represent the two ways in which a thing's essential nature can be defined. And, following Aristotle, essential definition is the means (as a middle term) of almost all strict demonstration, which is when, from necessary and universal premises, a conclusion necessarily follows, affirming an attribute of a subject: in the standard example of Aristotle, the eclipse of the sun.

The interest of Ockham's position is the exclusiveness with which he interprets demonstrative knowledge and the means of attaining it through essential definition. He effectively confines it to what can be inferred through self-evident, or analytic, propositions where knowledge of the meaning of the terms immediately brings assent. Like Scotus, Ockham interprets essential definition in a logical sense of what can be essentially affirmed of a subject—as "rational animal" can be affirmed of man—but unlike Duns, Ockham makes it exclusively of individual likeness and denies the possibility of analogy at all. A universal term is either of one concept or several; any comparison between them can only be among—equivocal —concepts standing for individual beings: in other words, there cannot be different logical and ontological levels of discourse: they must both refer to the same—individual—reality. More important, however, Ockham poses the problem of universal and necessary knowledge in a new way, namely, that if evidence can only be of what is known to exist immediately in intuitive knowledge, or is reducible to such knowledge, and all existence, other than God's, is contingent, how can evident knowledge give necessary knowledge? That was perhaps his single greatest philosophical legacy to his successors. It introduced a new awareness of the limitations of logical certainty to which the theories of Nicholas of Autrecourt, John of Mirecourt, or Buridan, among others, can be seen as the response. What has so often been taken as fourteenth-century skepticism was in fact an attempt to come to terms with a problem of which the thirteenth century seemed oblivious. It arose in the absence of inner illumination or some other means of ontological certainty, beyond individual existence. Duns, as we have discussed, had already taken the first step in seeking certainty logically by the four modes mentioned earlier. But for him, unlike Ockham, evidence did not depend exclusively upon intuitive knowledge.

Ockham's response was anything but agnostic. It was that a proposition could only be necessarily certain if it were removed from the mode of existence—which must always be contingent—to the mode of possibility. Thus to say "Every man is capable of laughter" is a contingent proposition because man need not exist; but to say "If a man exists, he is capable of laughter" is necessary because the capacity to laugh is an essential property of all men (by the second essential mode of definition where man is included in the definition of laughter). The whole of Ockham's intricate discussion of demonstration, principally in the third part of the *Logic,* is devoted to stating the conditions for universal and necessary propositions which can serve as premises in demonstrations, and to establishing how the different elements—of subject, its essential definition, and attribute—can be known. In each case the demonstrable must begin from the indemonstrable, which for Ockham as for Aristotle is what is immediately given in experience. Hence, for Ockham existence can never be demonstrated; it must be known intuitively, which, among other reasons, is why God's existence cannot be demonstrated, since he is naturally unknowable. Accordingly, the problem in all demonstration is to distinguish the demonstrable from the indemonstrable and to qualify out of existence what is indemonstrable either by making it tautological or in some other way self-evident, as in the proposition "Everything hot is heat-giving" which is self-evident in presupposing prior intuitive knowledge of the proposition "All heat is heat-giving" which, in turn, can only be known in experience and so is not necessary; or, alternatively, by making it conditional or hypothetical in introducing "whenever" or "if," in which case what follows will only be conditionally, and not universally, necessary. Demonstrability is thus restricted to what can be deduced from what is already known intuitively.

Not surprisingly few propositions fulfill these requirements, so that the number of strictly demonstrable propositions becomes with Ockham drastically reduced; much of his argument with his predecessors, especially Duns Scotus, is over the inadequacy of their criteria of a demonstration, so that what they regarded as necessarily true was only at most probable and often merely a persuasion, whose force was rhetorical rather than logical. That, however, has nothing to do with a restriction upon knowledge itself, or indeed skepticism towards what is known, but solely with what can be shown to hold universally and necessarily. Nor does knowledge thereby lose its universal character but simply its logical invariability as necessarily always being the case. These limitations come from the very pre-eminence of intuitive knowledge, from which not even mathematics are excluded, although, in being of what does not exist independently in nature, its propositions, especially those of geometry, are demonstrable; for demonstration depends upon establishing the necessary and universal logical conditions which hold for beings which ontologically are neither necessary nor universal. The problem is precisely to disclose those conditions and when and how they arise.

From one aspect Ockham's attitude to logical certainty, far from being the work of iconoclasm, was a valiant effort to preserve Aristotle's doctrine from the logic of his, Ockham's, own fundamentally different—Christian and individual—notion of being. More clearly than any other scholastic he showed the limitations of demonstration in a contingent world, which could only in certain instances be overcome by qualifying the meaning of propositions out of actual existence. The result was a redefinition of the role of demonstration to what could not be known in existence but must be known from existence. If its repercussions upon the prevailing metaphysical assumptions were far-reaching, in retrospect they could be said not to have been radical enough; for however far, epistemologically and ontologically, Ockham was prepared to go, in logic, as in his view of nature, he remained bound by Aristotle's system. Rather than discard Aristotle's principles he largely rendered his assumptions of both demonstration—that only necessary and universal knowledge was strict knowledge—and of the physical world—that all being was regulated by certain organizing metaphysical principles—inefficacious. An individual ontology answered to neither.

The overwhelming effect of Ockham's outlook was to substitute a physical explanation of the world and a logical explanation of knowledge of it for a metaphysical explanation of both. That is perhaps the reason why he had such difficulty in deciding what concepts were; for granted that they were a mental response to what was known, whether within or outside the intellect—in characteristically Christian style he attached the greatest certainty of all to inner self-knowledge—were they to be regarded as images of what was known, his initial response, or as acts of understanding of what was already known, his later position? For the presence of universal images seemed to introduce an intermediate layer between the intellect and its object; and on grounds of economy he came to reject them. More germane, although never explicit, is that metaphysics as an independent order of knowledge, a *scientia*, is effectively discarded. For if all being is individual, and the more common term, whether the subject of a body of knowledge or a concept, does not, as Ockham in each case insists against the contrary view of Duns Scotus, contain virtually knowledge of what comes under it, neither can yield knowledge of particular beings, whether as the study of being, which is the domain of metaphysics, or as the first adequate object of the intellect: with Ockham the concept of adequation, in the old scholastic axiom that knowledge is the adequation of the intellect with the thing, disappears and is displaced by similarity.

Now metaphysics is, with logic, the universalizing science. Where logic is the instrument of all the other sciences—in the sense of *scientiae* as separate bodies of knowledge with their own subject and conclusions as in physics, mathematics, medicine, and so on—metaphysics is designed to provide their principles. Whether or not it was fortuitous, Ockham did not write a separate work on metaphysics, whereas he wrote seven logical treatises and at least two, probably three, on physics. Like Duns Scotus, and unlike Aristotle and Aquinas, he did not conceive the different modes of physical being, such as the relation of potentiality and actuality, form and matter, under metaphysics; but, unlike Scotus, Ockham did not seek to transcend being's individual determinations, which were the province of the different sciences like physics, just because all being in this world could only be explained individually as existing in space and time and according to the other ten categories. Ockham therefore cut the ontological link between the individual and common natures or universal essences, uniting beings only conceptually in a transcendental term yielding knowledge of nothing and included in knowledge of nothing else. Hence the five predicables and the ten categories lost their metaphysical status and became logical terms of first and second intention according to whether they stood immediately for concepts—as genus, species, and the other predicables do—or for real things as the categories—substance, quality, quantity, and the others—do. Ockham thereby reduced all significative terms to the same individual import and made their differences as terms exclusively logical and grammatical.

What, then, remained to metaphysics? It is not a question Ockham ever directly raised; but in an instructive passage in his *Logic*, he affirms that the principles governing any real science—i.e., of real things—can be known either together with logic or under metaphysics. Thus, given a proper knowledge of a science and of logic, the conclusions deriving from such knowledge could, he says, easily be reached. That clearly suggests that the particular sciences together with logic can serve the same purpose traditionally ascribed to metaphysics, of combining universal understanding with knowledge of specific being. Metaphysics is thereby reduced to a merely conceptual role as the—traditional—repository for categories that can only be explained logically and physically in relation to actual individual being, which is the way in which Ockham treated them. The relation of metaphysical being to physical being thereby becomes logical instead of ontological, with the consequence that metaphysics lost any defined area not occupied by logic or the sciences of nature. Although Ockham continued to call metaphysics the science of being, its effective demise was the inescapable consequence of denying any identity to being beyond individuals. Logic became the one universalizing science standing above particular knowledge. Far from displacing metaphysics by nominalism, logic is the guarantee that the universal meaning of what is known can be reconciled with the individual nature of what exists. In that lay the beginning of a new approach which in the end was to displace the medieval outlook.

The major effect of Ockham's outlook was to redefine scholastic discourse, both in relation to knowledge and belief. After him the main philosophical and logical issues were precisely the scope and limits of knowledge and certainty, in the ways indicated in the first chapter. This shift in direction, rather than the divisions to which it gave rise between the Old and the New Ways—which has always tended to be made the focus of subsequent development—seems to me to be what is significant. It also brings proportion to what appear to be the extremities of thinkers like Nicholas of Autrecourt and John of Mirecourt, whose opinions were censured at Paris University in 1346 and 1347, respectively.

The interest of Autrecourt,[8] for long miscalled the Hume of the Middle

8. For Autrecourt see J. R. Weinberg, *Nicolaus of Autrecourt* (Princeton, 1965); *The Universal Treatise of Nicholas of Autrecourt*, trans. L. A. Kennedy, R. E. Arnold, A. E. Millward (Milwaukee, 1971); and P. Vignaux, "Nicholas d'Autrecourt," *Dictionnaire de Théologie Catholique* (Paris, 1931), 11: 562–87.

Ages, is that he applied the same criteria of evident knowledge of incomplexes—terms and things immediately known—to propositions and demonstrations; namely, that what was not immediately known was not evidential. There were no degrees of certainty. That left nothing but the principle of contradiction—that the same proposition cannot be affirmed and denied at the same time. He thereby rejected the way of causality to prove one proposition from another. That was not the same as denying causality but merely its certainty. Autrecourt still admitted a real relation between cause and effect known evidently; he merely denied its self-evident, or analytical, certainty. Nor like Hume did he reduce a relation simply to a psychological habit of associating one thing with another. His position was an extension of Ockham's: it arose from the problem posed by Ockham that all evidence begins from experience of existence by the senses, but nothing known evidently is certain (because it is contingent). Noncontradiction provided the one source of certainty. All propositions must be reducible to it directly or indirectly. Where Autrecourt does show some affinity with Hume is in accepting that appearances alone do not give truth, so that a false opinion could appear more probable than its contradictory just because it is not analytically certain. Autrecourt's singularity does not end there. It is also to be seen in his reliance upon final cause alone, and his rejection of the other three causes, in reaching even probable conclusions. It went with, at the time, an equally unique rejection of Aristotle, not only in epistemology but also in cosmology. To Autrecourt the principle of good is the end, or final cause, of everything: something exists because it is good that it should do so. Without such a principle there would be no reason for anything among the infinity of possible things. Its accompaniment was an equally unusual doctrine of atomism, which dispensed with anything, absolute or relative, beyond the individual things which are related. That, too, can be seen as an extension of Ockham's view that movement, like the other seven categories after substance and quality, is simply a nominal definition, meaning here something which is successively in different places. Unlike Autrecourt, however, Ockham kept within an Aristotelian framework though changing its real import. For Autrecourt, on the other hand, such local movement is the only kind of movement, while the generation and destruction of bodies is due not to the introduction and displacement of forms—Aristotle's doctrine—but to the combination and disintegration of the atoms constituting everything. Again the principle of the good as the unifying principle of the universe leads to the belief in the eternity of things as part of its perfection, with each thing having its own inner principle.

There was little or nothing, then, of the skeptic in Autrecourt, certainly not in the negative pejorative sense in which it is usually applied to the thinkers of this period. Nor can his singularities be attributed to Ockham. They came from a radical empiricism unharnessed from the accepted mediation of Aristotle and allied to a syncretism of epicurean and platonic concepts. Nevertheless, it is within the context of Ockham's outlook that the empiricism which led to the unharnessing must be understood.

John of Mirecourt is more directly in the Ockhamist tradition, in his epistemology and in his ethics, and has none of Autrecourt's strange cosmology, although both were condemned among other things for saying that God could command someone to hate him, which, if done in dependence upon God's will, would not be sin or error by the creature doing it. In Mirecourt's case that came from identifying what God wills efficaciously —the way he concurs in any created act—with his approbation, so that whatever God permits, he also wills. That standpoint was also adopted by Thomas of Bradwardine but from an entirely opposite position of depreciating the intrinsic worth of any human or created action.

The problem raised by Autrecourt and Mirecourt was the same as that earlier mentioned in connection with Scotus; namely, that actions are good or bad because God wills them such. But Duns had not gone beyond stating that as a proposition. Ockham had largely followed Scotus, making the one absolute ethical constant love of God above all, which by definition excluded the ability of someone to hate him; for although God could command such an act without contradiction, to obey it would involve a contradiction in at once loving him above all—in doing his will—and hating him. That illustrates the absurdity to which the ethical implications of Scotus and Ockham could lead: for God is then involved in the contradiction of commanding what is contradictory. In general it means that a precept is itself not contradictory but the obligation to obey it is. In Ockham's as in Scotus's case, there is an irreconcilable tension between the existing moral order governed by God's commandments and the precepts of right reason on the one hand, and their contingency in God's power to override them on the other. Even though neither thinker attempted to pursue it, and Ockham even more than Scotus insisted upon the conformity of volition with right reason as the indispensable condition of any virtuous act, the gap between what held *de facto* and what could be by God's absolute power was there for others to pursue. They did so mostly in the way mentioned earlier. The arbitrariness of their conclusions was accentuated by Ockham's refusal to accept any formal distinction between God's attributes—of intellect, will, mercy, goodness, and so on—which all became connotative terms signifying God in his absolute simplicity knowing or willing or showing his goodness or mercy to his creatures. That tended to reduce the equation between them to the relation between God's will in its absolute freedom and free will which could act for good or bad under God's direct impulsion: how it acted depended upon whether, with Scotus and Ockham, whatever God willed could not be bad, and so he could not be the direct cause of sin as sin, or whether he could be its direct cause and, because it was from him, it would not be the created will's fault, the position of their successors like Autrecourt and Mirecourt. Either way it meant blurring, and indeed, reversing distinctions central to moral theology. The wheel had come full circle from the inexorability of the Latin Averroists.

At the same time the application of Ockham's analytical principles to theology led to comparable difficulties, especially in denying strict meaning to propositions which had no literal signification. In 1340, the university authorities at Paris, having in the previous year issued a general admonition against the preaching of Ockham's doctrines, expressly prohibited the practice in the arts faculty of taking the literal sense of a proposition as false or denying the reality of words like "Socrates" or "God" or "creature," because they did not immediately stand for anything real in personal supposition, an assertion later attributed to Nicholas of Autrecourt.[9] These practices, too, the authorities associated with Ockham's name, although against precisely whom they were directed is unclear.

Buridan was rector of the arts faculty at the time. He again must be understood in the context of Ockham's doctrines, independently of whether or not he actively opposed those censured in 1340. His logic is also

9. For a detailed analysis of the implications of the statute, see R. Paqué, *Der Pariser Nominalistenstatut* (Berlin, 1970).

the logic of terminism. But he is not really an Ockhamist there or else-where. In logic he allowed more autonomy to terms and propositions, locating the truth of the paradox of the liar in its own form as a statement about something which is the case. At the same time he moved further away from the classical Aristotelian conception of demonstration as the summit of knowledge, while rejecting Autrecourt's reduction of certainty to the principle of contradiction for restricting what is true to evidence of existence.

Yet it may be doubted whether they were talking about the same thing. For Buridan, unlike Autrecourt and Ockham, evidence in that sense does not seem to have been the basis of truth. Autrecourt's problem was pre-cisely how to derive certainty from appearances in default of intuitive knowledge of their certainty. His arguments directed against a certain Bernard of Arezzo, whose opinions survive only in Autrecourt's two surviv-ing letters to him,[10] were that to assume, with Bernard, that intuitive knowledge is only what is judged to exist but that God could, but does not, cause it to be of what does not exist, is to destroy any means of evidence. For it makes evident knowledge depend upon what cannot be evident, namely, that God does not intervene to make intuitive knowledge illusory. Contrary to Ockham, therefore, whom Autrecourt does not criticize, Ber-nard divorced the possibility of intuitive knowledge from knowledge of nonexistents, thereby removing Ockham's condition for its evidentiality. To Autrecourt that was to deny the basis of any knowledge. Unlike Ock-ham, however, he did not restore Ockham's safeguard of making intuitive knowledge equally of existence and nonexistents; he departed from the naive realism, in the modern sense, of intuitive knowledge altogether, and instead of assuming God's direct intervention, adduced probable argu-ments to disprove it. Only if it is accepted that God does not induce knowledge of nonexistents is knowledge possible naturally at all. But that also entails accepting the reality of appearances and dispensing with the notion of a special, intuitive, psychic awareness of existence as the basis for evident judgments of existence. Evidence, then, lies in judgments made over what in every case appears to be the case and not in degrees of

10. Translated in H. Shapiro (ed.), *Medieval Philosophy: Select Readings from Augustine to Buridan* (New York, 1964), pp. 510–26.

certainty over what is apprehended. That was effectively to displace simple knowledge as immediately of existence for inferential knowledge reached as a judgment of assent to what is believed to be true. The only certainty is thereby the logical certainty of noncontradiction, which excludes the contradictory of what is assented to. Without that assurance, in a world where all appearances must be taken as equally true, they must be taken as equally probable. Error correspondingly arises where a judgment actually exceeds the appearance someone has.

Leaving aside the bizarre consequences that this attitude had, it nevertheless shared with Ockham the common assumption that what is known is evidently true, however tenuous such evidence is.

Buridan,[11] on the other hand, from the predominantly naturalistic standpoint of one who devoted his intellectual career to the study of the arts—philosophy, logic, and nature—although conceding as a Christian that God could intervene in knowledge, as in nature, was not concerned with the implications for either, nor, it seems, with evidence as the source of knowledge. In both his epistemology and his logic he accepted the validity of concepts, terms, and propositions in their own right, without recourse to the experience of the senses. Far from beginning from what can be known through them intuitively—Buridan makes no use of the notion of intuitive knowledge—the senses can be deluded, and it is the intellect which corrects them. Hence all knowledge is not dependent upon the senses. The very fact that we have a simple concept of substance must mean that substances are known directly, in opposition to Nicholas of Autrecourt's denial on the grounds that substance cannot be distinguished from its accidents. Again, universals not only signify the individuals coming under them; they also represent them in their universality as genus and species, a position superficially cognate with Duns Scotus's.

In logic, Buridan dispensed with simple supposition, going further than Ockham in dissociating meaning from any real correspondence with things. A proposition taken for itself is a sentence and nothing more, a grouping of words whose truth lies in the supposition of its terms, not their significa-

11. The difference between Autrecourt and Buridan has recently been discussed by T. K. Scott, "Nicholas of Autrecourt, Buridan and Ockhamism," *Journal of the History of Philosophy* 9(1971): 15–41. For Buridan's logic see J. Buridan, *Sophisms on Meaning and Truth*, trans. T. K. Scott (New York, 1966).

tion. Buridan took issue with Gregory of Rimini's contention that propositions like terms signify their own reality, which Gregory called a proposition's total significate; or as it has become more commonly known, a complex, as opposed to a simple, signifiable: that is, an abstract whole which is real although it does not actually exist as such, in the way that the proposition "Man is an animal" has a real counterpart in man as an animal or in its equivalent form "man being an animal."

To Buridan that was merely to hypostasize propositions and was against the whole tendency of his logic, if not his outlook as a whole. Much has been made of the complex signifiable, one modern writer seeing it as the beginning of modern thought.[12] It also engaged, among others, Robert Holcot and Walter Chatton over the question of what was the object of knowledge and belief, Holcot holding to Ockham's and Buridan's position that it was a proposition's conclusion, and Chatton that it was its signification. That, in turn, goes back to Ockham's opposition to Duns Scotus's claim that the subject of a proposition contained virtually knowledge of its attribute and conclusion, which Gregory of Rimini extended, in turn, to the claim by Ockham that it was the conclusion, on similar grounds, that the conclusion does not presuppose knowledge of the subject and attribute.[13] The complex signifiable was an attempt to combine the signification of all of them in one total significate. Even if only to a limited extent, it was a regression from the logic of terms and propositions to the older belief that logic was concerned with extramental reality, though not in this case actual existence. As such, it can hardly be regarded as a fundamental development in the change from a medieval outlook. Rather, it is one among the issues concerned with the ramifications of knowledge.

Each of these thinkers bears witness in different ways to those issues, as well as, in the case of Autrecourt and Mirecourt, to their implications for theology; and all of them, except for Chatton, were in some manner influenced by Ockham's ideas. To call them Ockhamist, however, and to

12. H. Elie, *Le Complexe Significabile* (Paris, 1937). For a more recent assessment see E. A. Moody, *"A Quodlibetal* Question of Robert Holcot O. P., on the Problem of the Objects of Knowledge and Belief," *Speculum* 39(1964): 53–74.

13. See G. Leff, *Gregory of Rimini: Tradition and Innovation in Fourteenth Century Thought* (Manchester, 1961), pp. 52–61. Also G. Leff, *Bradwardine and the Pelagians* (Cambridge, 1957) and F. Hoffmann, *Die Theologische Methode des Oxforder Dominikanerlehrers Robert Holcot* (Münske, 1971) and bibliography therein.

oppose them to those who opposed Ockham, like Bradwardine, Burley, or Chatton, or remained largely unaffected by him doctrinally, as many of those mentioned earlier in connection with the Scotist view of created grace were, would be to seek the same kind of conformity with an independent abstract reality which Gregory of Rimini sought in the complex signifiable. None of those just mentioned, or any others, with the possible exception of Adam of Woodham, was an adherent of Ockham in all essentials: Mirecourt rejects intuitive knowledge of nonexistents; so does Holcot, who also takes a more favorable view of theology's status as a body of knowledge. Autrecourt is an aberrant, whose own demotion of the status of the propositions he defends to no more than probable and his anti-Aristotelianism, which is the driving force of his outlook, contradict the whole profoundly serious, nonagnostic intent of Ockham's. Buridan and Gregory of Rimini converge and diverge with almost dizzying shifts: Buridan, in logic an extreme terminist, in epistemology and nature seems to have been a Realist and metaphysician as well as free from any association with God's absolute power, in knowledge, nature or ethics; Gregory of Rimini follows Ockham's division of simple knowledge into intuitive and abstractive, accepts God's intervention in knowledge, nature and grace, and yet evinces little or no concern with terminist logic, upholds both sensible and intelligible species, and opposes the slightest concession to human worth in contradistinction to both Scotus's and Ockham's tendency to exalt man's capacity for virtue.

But beyond any such catalogue, which it would be tedious and repetitious to pursue, lies the fundamental consideration that these thinkers like any other group were operating within their own distinct milieu. However much they were responding to their predecessors they were doing so in terms of their own debates and alignments, often to the neglect and distortion, and nearly always in modification, of the ideas that prompted them; thus, in Buridan's opposition to Autrecourt it may be doubted whether either thinker, particularly Buridan, had Ockham in mind at all: Buridan was rebutting Autrecourt, and Autrecourt, Bernard of Arezzo, each in favor of his own, not Ockham's, version of the truth. Even Holcot's reaffirmation of Ockham's standpoint over the object of knowledge had a different import, in being directed against the complex signifiable of Gregory of Rimini, where Ockham's originally had originally been the Scotist notion of virtual knowledge. That is to say, the very discontinuities between different contexts involve discontinuities even within the same doctrine. When an outlook is itself in gestation, as it was during the middle decades of the fourteenth century, the direct affinities are even more tenuous.

Rather than attempt, therefore, to make such affinities and oppositions between pedigrees and schools the intellectual measure, it is more germane to locate it in the dominant intellectual issues, attitudes and activities taken as a whole. Together they provide the framework in which to place the different pursuits and doctrines and thereby the role of the thinkers involved: it makes more sense to see Nicholas of Autrecourt not as a representative or traducer of Ockhamism but as someone concerned with the nature of evidence who sought to interpret it in a new way.

So far as the period from the 1330s to the 1360s is concerned, the main issues were a refinement and development of those raised principally by Scotus and Ockham as we have already considered them, namely, the nature of evidence; the object of knowledge; the status of theology; the universals and individuals; God's omnipotence and the relation of his will to free will over grace, merit, sin, and future contingents; and a range of theological-cum-physical questions connected with change, the intensification and remission of forms, movement, quantity, substance, and accidents, most of which figured in Ockham's doctrine of the eucharist, articles from which were included among the fifty-one censured at Avignon in 1327. These questions received a new prominence, and in the case of future contingents a new form, by applying logic to revelation in a way eschewed by Ockham, namely, by pursuing the implications of two contradictory propositions: that the future is contingent and that God knows everything determinately. It led to the impasse, the consequences of which have been mentioned in passing before, of opposing omniscience to revelation, so that either, in the case of Adam of Woodham and Thomas Buckingham, God in knowing everything, including the future as free and contingent, is liable to know what may not occur, and so his revelation of the future could be falsified, thereby misleading Christ and the faithful. Alternatively, in order to preserve the certainty of God's knowledge, it is excluded from what has yet to be and may not come to be: the path of Holcot and earlier of Aureole and Durandus. Posed in that way, the issue of future contingents is the supreme example of the logicizing of theology; it extended the logical analysis of theological truths begun by Ockham to one of the mysteries—together with the Trinity—from which he had expressly excluded the possibility of logical resolution. Future contingents thus epitomize in general the development of a mode of thinking beyond the prescribed limits of its founder, and in particular the logic of the contingency of the universe. On both counts they represent more than mere Ockhamism.

It is this new logicizing spirit within the framework of a contingent world that is the hallmark of the fourteenth-century outlook. It embraced theology, knowledge, nature, and logic itself. Its products were therefore as diverse as the subjects themselves. Neither logical terminism nor the theology of God's omnipotence was the preserve of any one school, nor are they an index of radicalism. Together they formed the poles of intellectual discourse. Only when harnessed to an individual ontology can they be called Ockhamist. But it was precisely the variety of application that accounts for the intellectual pluralism of the fourteenth century, both in the same thinker and in the different intellectual pursuits. Ockham, apart from Nicholas of Cusa, was the last systematizer of the Middle Ages, and his was a system to end system. He succeeded only too well. Within a decade of his outlook there was no longer an overarching theology or noetic within which enquiry was pursued: theology, philosophy, logic, mathematics, and physical knowledge were all going their own way, often in the same thinker, as we have remarked in the cases of, say, Buridan or Burley whose nominalism in logic did not prevent their upholding a realist epistemology, while Autrecourt could reach a degree of skepticism about what was certain, as opposed to what could be known probably, from an ontology that was closer to a world of Platonic forms than almost anyone since perhaps John Scotus in the ninth century. Yet he is only stating in a more extreme manner the new logical recognition, born of awareness that at the natural level most knowledge is contingent and never more than probable, while by God's power, supernaturally, whatever is not contradictory is possible. Probability and possibility, so widespread in the fourteenth century, are thus the accompaniment of a changed way of looking at the world, not skepticism about it.

That is where the dissolution came: in removing the old categories and with them the old certainties. The Christian assumptions remained unimpaired, but they were being put to a new meaning, which in nearly every case involved emancipation from what could not be actually ascertained by human experience or scientific enquiry or derived from logic or need be held on faith. That left them unmediated by metaphysics and natural theology, whether in the direct relation of free will to God's will over created grace and future contingents, or the terms and propositions taken formally for themselves in logic, or the direct rapport between subject and object in knowledge, or in the attention to the measurable and verifiable in nature. The speculation that accompanied them remained undiminished, but it was directed into new channels away from the universal mediation of abstract realities that until then had dominated the medieval conception of the world and man's relation to it and to their creator. Imperceptibly for those involved, but decisively for the future, the unitary mold of the past enclosing men from direct contact with what lay outside them was being broken, bringing them into the presence of a new diversity in nature and a new freedom in their conception of God. If the immediate effect was intellectual babel in the ways we have been remarking, it was also the confusion of new awareness, which it needed three centuries to develop into coherent alternatives. We must now consider some of their beginnings in nature.

III. The Physical World

As we have said, there is a comparable displacement of the categories of nature in the fourteenth century. Here the revision was of Aristotle's physics and, more indirectly, his cosmology. Correspondingly it arose not through any conscious attempt to overthrow his system in its natural as opposed to supernatural aspect, as a physical explanation of physical phenomena; but, as so often with new developments, in the effort to save or strengthen his explanations from apparent anomalies. Aristotle continued to provide the terms of physical inquiry until his demise in the new mechanistic universe of the seventeenth century. But it was in the fourteenth century that they first underwent the reinterpretation that, after an interval of two and a half centuries, was to be instrumental in that greater change.

Much has been made of the impact of Christian conceptions upon the new scientific thinking of the fourteenth century, which sometimes tends to be regarded as the expression of the changes we have just been considering in philosophy and theology. To make them too direct, however, would be to misconceive their relationship. To begin with, it is important to retain the distinction just mentioned between Aristotle as the philosopher of nature and of what lies beyond nature. It was only the second that came under attack in 1277 in offering an alternative non-Christian interpretation of reality. Over the first, as an account of how the universe operated physically, and—with modifications—of its constituents, Aristotle's authority, and indeed that of Averroës as his principal commentator for the Christian West, remained virtually unimpaired. It was therefore common for them to be opposed on one count and invoked on the other, as thinker after thinker did, without implying inconsistency or the schizophrenic tendencies that the more psychoanalytically inclined have detected in the fourteenth-century mentality, whatever that may be. The increased awareness of the different levels of discourse, which *is* one of the characteristics of the period, applied as much to authorities, as we have remarked in their overzealous application to the words of the Bible censured at Paris in 1340, as it did to what was under discussion.

In the second place, some of the most important developments in the fourteenth century, notably that over the existence of a void and the cause of projectile movement, have their origin directly from an earlier period beginning, as in this case, often with John of Philipon's criticism of Aristotle's principles in the sixth century.[1] That also holds for the one initially genuine theological problem, of the intensification and remission of forms, first posed in the *Sentences* of Peter Lombard over the manner in which created grace as a form in the soul was increased or decreased. By the middle of the thirteenth century it had been extended to the question of how physical forms in general, such as heat or cold or whiteness, became more or less intense. As such it was treated mathematically in the fourteenth century.

For that reason, we must beware positing too close a correlation of a theological or philosophical standpoint with physical conceptions. By the end of the thirteenth century, the main scientific questions that were to engage the attention of the fourteenth century had been formulated, even if they were subsequently to be reformulated. They therefore provided a common point of departure, which largely overlaid their origins in a particular view of reality. That is true of small and great differences alike, including the fundamental divergence between an Augustinian and an Aris-

1. For the background as well as general accounts of scientific development in the Middle Ages, see A. C. Crombie, *Medieval and Early Modern Science*, 2 vols. (New York, 1958) and E. J. Dijksterhuis, *The Mechanisation of the World Picture* (Oxford, 1969) and bibliographies therein.

totelian notion of the source of truth. The Augustinian Platonic stress upon its intelligible nonsensory nature had led Robert Grosseteste, as it had led Plato, to see in mathematics the one kind of certain knowledge accessible to man naturally, and to the application of mathematics to a new form of physical theory based upon light. The greatest advances in mathematics in the thirteenth and earlier fourteenth centuries had been among his successors at Oxford, above all, Robert Kilwardby and Thomas Bradwardine, who had combined their study with a more traditional Augustinian outlook. Through Bradwardine the mathematical tradition was passed on to his Mertonian successors, while at Paris in the 1350s and 1360s Nicholas of Oresme was the greatest exponent of mathematics in physics. But none of these later thinkers combined it with the pursuit of an Augustinian metaphysics, as indeed Bradwardine had not. The problems to which they addressed themselves were all of a strictly physical, nonphilosophical kind, as we shall mention in due course. Their use of mathematics was for the solution of problems which had by then become detached from the original conceptions which had helped to frame them. They were no longer the preserve of a particular philosophical or theological outlook.

Now this detachment of physical theory from a predominantly metaphysical and theological context, in which it had been subordinated to wider metaphysical and theological issues, was the condition of its independent development; it enabled physical problems to be treated in their own terms by specifically physical and mathematical considerations and not as instances to illustrate metaphysical or theological questions, such as the relation of form to matter or substances to accidents or God's power to separate one from the other. That involved a loosening of the ties with both theology and the predominantly speculative and metaphysical approach of Aristotelian physics and cosmology.

The separation of fourteenth-century science from either must not however be made too sharp. With nature, as with logic, there had been an independent tradition since at least the beginning of the twelfth century, with its own distinct genre of scientific treatises, especially on astronomy and light, and individuals like Adelard of Bath in the twelfth century and Witelo in the thirteenth who devoted themselves almost wholly to the study of natural phenomena. Nor did fourteenth-century scientific thinkers like Bradwardine or Buridan confine themselves to science, while the majority, such as most of the names mentioned in the previous chapter, including Ockham and the so-called Ockhamists, continued to treat scientific problems speculatively and philosophically rather than scientifically. The difference was rather that in the fourteenth century, for the first time, a distinctive body scientific, mainly mechanical, theory arose with its own independent principles and procedures, which were self-contained and not subservient to higher nonphysical principles. It arose from the quantitative treatment, through the application of mathematics and up to a point logic, of problems which until then had been considered qualitatively under their different categories of movement, time, place, quantity, and quality.

These new quantitative methods mark the beginnings, albeit inchoate, of future scientific procedure, namely, in generalizing the conclusions arrived at by calculation or analysis as formulae or laws to be taken as axioms on the Euclidean model and applied to physical phenomena. Kepler, Galileo, and their contemporaries adopted a number of them. What, however, these early attempts lacked was any attempt at empirical investigation or confirmation. They were not at that time compensated by adequate methods of calculation or measurement. They were the brave attempts to create the foundations of physical explanation in the absence of any common stock of testable scientific theories or the requisite mathematical and empirical means to support them.

As such, they mark a new stage in the interpretation of physical phenomena and the role of mathematics in their explanation. That did not come near to constituting an alternative physics and cosmology, but was rather a series of efforts at new modes of problem-solving within the existing assumptions. The representatives of the two main schools of the Mertonians and Parisians involved lacked any intention of framing new hypotheses about the nature or even the cause of what they were investigating or indeed any conception of such investigation as the interplay of hypothesis and data. Nor did they see themselves as engaged in a distinctive activity differentiating them as scientists. They continued to take as given the categories and definitions handed down from Aristotle, whose texts still largely formed the framework of the arts course within which they operated. That can be seen in one of the most influential products of the Mertonian school, William of Heytesbury's *Rules for Solving Sophisms* (fallacies), which was designed as a textbook for first-year students in logic;

the strongly mathematical character of some of its questions exemplifies the close and novel connection between physics, logic, and mathematics in a new quantitative relation, as we shall mention again. It was just this incorporation of those new elements into the traditional structure which differentiated these fourteenth-century thinkers from their predecessors.

The divergence was above all in mode of approach, away from the predominantly qualitative and classificatory conception of Aristotle[2] and the Aristotelian tradition to one directed to physical problems defined in terms of the material attributes of bodies—quantity, weight, quality, dimensions—and treated quantitatively. It meant the substitution of a generalizing method based upon measurement—principally of movement in place and time—for a conceptualizing one based upon definition which is then analyzed into its constituent elements, in the way that Aristotle's treatment of movement started from his definition of it "as the fulfillment of the movable *qua* movable, the cause of the attribute being contact with the movable"; and then proceeded to distinguish between the four different kinds of movement—substantial change, qualitative alteration, change in quantity, and local movement—each in turn defined by its own qualities, and all united under the universal principle that whatever is moved is moved by something else. Once such a classification has been established all movement must come under it, made explicable by reference to one or other of its different modes, which was why, among other things, Aristotelian mechanics could not account for changes in acceleration or accept the existence of a void or comprehend the law of inertia. These all fell outside or were excluded from one or the other of its definitions, which in being taken for a true account of reality could not extend to include what could not be subsumed under them, or contradicted them, as the principle of inertia, that something can persist in a state of motion—or rest—unless disturbed, lay outside the Aristotelian axiom that everything is moved by something else; and the existence of a void is contradicted by the Aristotelian definition that the velocity of a moving body is directly proportional to the resistance of the medium (air) in which it moves, so that in

2. For an enlightening analysis of Aristotle's scientific approach and its legacy see E. McMullin, ed., *The Concept of Matter in Greek and Medieval Philosophy* (Notre Dame, 1965), pp. 178–81.

a void, where there would be no resistance, movement would be instantaneous, a conclusion dismissed by Aristotle as absurd and therefore impossible. Movement and, similarly, all the other definable phenomena of the physical world, whether matter or form, time or space, thus become identified with particular attributes that distinguish them qualitatively from one another. And scientific inquiry becomes the correct application of their definitions and classifications. However well founded empirically the initial observations leading to them may have been, and that is precisely what distinguished Aristotle from Plato, having been formulated they are then treated as autonomous. What should have at best been an explanatory hypothesis, and more often was merely a definition, was taken as an axiom from which all subsequent conclusions can be deduced.

This classificatory method applied to nature could only create a barrier to proper scientific knowledge and discovery, for it enclosed physical enquiry, which must, by definition, begin from and be regulated by what is observable and/or physically identifiable, in self-contained axioms and definitions. The natural world was thereby effectively shut out, leaving Aristotle and his successors with only the conceptualizations formed from it. The original empirical element accordingly became fossilized in the abstractions that it had engendered, with no systematic interplay through experiment upon what lay outside them. For that reason Aristotle's physics are closer to metaphysics, with his own frequently acute personal observations and conclusions harnessed to an ontology of forms acting upon matter as the defining and actualizing agents in all being and change, which are conceived as the transformation of the potential into the actual. The resultant world of change and development was Aristotle's resolution of his version of the polarities characteristic of the Greek conception of reality. Unlike Plato, for whom the opposition was between ideal and appearance, the Aristotelian contrast between the potential (matter) and the actual (form) enabled him to locate the intelligible in the sensible as the repository of the forms constituting the true nature of everything. Moreover, since everything acts toward an end in the realization of its own nature, as a heavy body falling is seeking the earth as its natural resting place, there is a presiding teleology that makes the world intelligible.

Not surprisingly, such an approach to physical reality, together with a cosmology which made the center of the earth—surrounded concentrically by the four elements of earth, water, fire, and air, each with its own physical characteristics—the center of the universe, once it had taken hold, virtually ended independent physical enquiry in the proper empirical sense for the 2,000 years in which it was dominant. That independence was not restored in the fourteenth century. The thinkers with whom we are concerned certainly drew upon their observations to explain violent movement or acceleration; but these were not their principal means; nor did they submit their hypotheses and conclusions to anything that could be called experiment or verification. Their departure was to reformulate Aristotle's definitions and explanations in terms of matter and quantity and to resolve them by calculation as opposed to mere classification and definition.

How important that change was can be seen in a comparison with Ockham. Conceptually, he went further than anyone during the Middle Ages in reducing all being to individual being and all physical phenomena to the attributes of individual beings in their different aspects. Hence, as we discussed in the previous chapter, only material substance and physical qualities are real; all the other categories neither inhere in being nor stand for independent essences or things or forms, but merely describe in a nominal definition the different ways in which individual things can be said to exist, whether as extended in space (quantity) or in movement, where they are successively in different places, or in relation to other individual beings. Philosophically, Ockham, of all the scholastics, provided the clearest justification for opening the physical world to observation and experience for itself and not for something beyond it or within it. With the individual the sole measure of existence, there was no longer a being beyond individual being of which the individual was only the occasion; and since only physical being is real and absolute—in the sense of independently existing—being, it can only be considered by physics. Its concern is individual substance and quality as physical entities.

That represented philosophically the elimination of an entire realm of metaphysical abstraction, where terms like "being," "essence," "substance," "form," and "matter," either represent concepts (as what were called terms of second intention) when they belong to logic, or they stand directly for real things (as terms of first intention), in which case they come under physics as a real (first order) science. That did not however lead Ockham to anything that can be called a new scientific conception or method.

Unlike the Mertonians or Parisians or a conservative theologian and philosopher like Bradwardine, Ockham made no independent scientific contribution because he did not go beyond the level of conceptual, as opposed to physical or mathematical, abstraction. Movement, time, place, quantity, and the other categories remained concepts, physical concepts, it is true, defined in relation to actual individual beings, but not physical phenomena to be explained in terms of physical events. They therefore remained definitions of *what* something is, not explanations of how and why and in what conditions something behaves in certain ways—the point at which physical explanation begins. Ockham never reached it because his semantic and ontological preoccupations took him only as far as classification of meanings. That is not to minimize its philosophical importance; it is to distinguish what is philosophically significant from scientific significance: not only can they be distinct, but one may be an impediment to the other.

Each of these occurrences is apparent in Ockham's relation to the new scientific developments of the fourteenth century; they both arose from his radical simplification of ontological import, which, in not positing more than is necessary to explain the *philosophical* use of a concept or hypothesis, failed to do justice to its physical and scientific complexity. Two comparisons, one over a specific problem, the second of approach to nature and physical phenomena, may perhaps illustrate that.

The first concerns movement and its application to the problem of violent—called unnatural by Aristotle—movement, exemplified by a projectile, which in being thrown, is moved by an external impulsion. The question of what caused the continuance of that movement, after the initial impulsion, was hard to explain on Aristotelian principles, and had been a matter of debate well before the fourteenth century.[3] According to Aristotle, movement arose, as we have said, from the continuous action of the mover upon the moved, expressed in the principle that everything moved is moved by something else. The mover as the source of movement was for him a force—internal in natural movement, external in unnatural movement as in that of a projectile. In both cases movement continued only so long as the mover was in direct contact with the moved. Moreover, since

3. For the remainder of this chapter I am principally indebted to M. Clagett, *The Science of Mechanics in the Middle Ages* (Madison, 1961) and in the case of Heytesbury to C. Wilson, *William of Heytesbury: Medieval Logic and the Rise of Mathematical Physics* (Madison, 1956).

movement only occurs in time, it is also accompanied by resistance—the absence of which in a void was, it will be recalled, Aristotle's reason for rejecting a void's existence. Hence, in natural movement, where the force and time are constant, movement, or the distance covered, is inversely proportional to the resistance of the medium (air); in unnatural movement, so long as the force is sufficient to produce movement, and with the resistance constant, the movement will be directly proportional to the magnitude of the moving force. Aristotle supposed that in unnatural movement this moving force was transmitted to the air as the medium in which the object moved, so that it remains in motion after contact with the original mover, i.e., the hand throwing the stone or ball, has ceased because the air behind the projectile acts as mover, with each wave either being mutually replaced by the next as the projectile passes through it, or through the air also receiving the power or force to act as mover. Aristotle seems to have adopted the second explanation. John of Philipon rejected this view of the medium as the cause of movement and saw it instead in an impressed force imparted to that which was moved. But it was not until the end of the thirteenth century and the first decades of the fourteenth century that notion of impulsion through a force impressed into the object was revived, first through Olivi and then through Ockham's Franciscan confrere, and a follower of Scotus, Francis of Marchia, before it was given a definitive statement by Buridan, in which form it became the accepted solution for the rest of the Middle Ages, and for Galileo afterward. Where Olivi and Marchia had regarded the impressed force as transitory, Buridan treated it as a permanent quality called *impetus* (Galileo later used the same word, *impeto*). The significance of Buridan's explanation is that for the first time he conceived impetus not as communicated to the medium but to the matter of the body itself which is moving, expressed in the principle that the greater the mass a body has the further it can be projected. Its impetus will therefore vary both according to the velocity of the projectile and the quantity of matter of the moving body. Buridan said: "And by the amount the motor moves the moving body more swiftly, by the same amount it will impress in it a stronger impetus. . . . Hence by the amount more there is of matter, by that amount can the body receive more of that impetus and more intensely."[4] Here, then, although not expressed mathematically and

4. Clagett, *The Science of Mechanics in the Middle Ages*, pp. 522–23.

although no means were suggested of how the matter or the impetus could be measured, was an attempt at a quantitative formulation. As such it became the starting point for the numerous mathematical calculations based upon it among Buridan's Parisian successors. At the same time Buridan explained the cessation of violent movement by the debilitating resistance of the medium which gradually destroys the impulse: it is not, therefore, as it was for Aristotle, self-expending, and were it not for that resistance, it would continue uninterruptedly. Equally fruitful was Buridan's application of the principle of impetus to the acceleration of falling bodies produced, on this view, by the gravity of the body continually impressing more impetus which in turn increases the velocity of its fall, a formulation which approaches the later concept of momentum.

Leaving aside subsequent developments, what is noteworthy about Buridan's theory is first that it is arrived at on the Aristotelian premise that everything moved must be moved by something else, and hence by the need to find an accompanying mover for the moving projectile. And second, therefore, that far from simplifying the concept of movement by identifying it with *impetus*, it introduces the further concept of an impressed force, the precise nature of which, as opposed to the effect it has, Buridan was never able to specify. Although, therefore, this view could be said to approach the Newtonian principle of inertia in the condition—which holds for the heavenly bodies at the world's creation—that a thing's movement would continue indefinitely if there were no resistance, at the level of terrestrial mechanics, where it can never be fulfilled, it has no place for inertia. That is to say, both philosophically and mechanically its assumptions were antithetical to those very scientific developments toward which its consequences were to be so fruitful a contribution.

Now let us turn to Ockham for whom movement is nothing separate from a moving body, but a nominal definition stating that something is successively in different places. He accordingly rejected the Aristotelian assumption, although directing his criticism solely against his contemporaries, and not against Aristotle, of the need in projectile movement, as in any other, for a continuing moving force, and affirmed instead that it is moved by itself. His own words are indicative of his approach and mode of reasoning:

In the movement of a projectile there is a special difficulty over the moving cause and the effect of this movement since it cannot be the projecting force, which can cease to exist without the projectile ceasing to move. Nor can it be the air, because it can be moved in opposite directions, as it would be if an arrow and a stone were to meet, sent from opposite directions. Nor can the moving force be in the stone, because I ask by what it is caused. It cannot be by the projector, because a natural agent uniformly close to its object will uniformly cause the same effect. But a projector can be uniformly close to a stone and yet not move it, as when my hand moves something slowly it will not move it locally but when it moves it quickly it will move it locally. Therefore this moving force cannot be caused by anything absolute or relative in the projector nor by the projector's own movement, because local movement never causes an effect unless the agent is in contact with the object, as has been often said before. But that can equally apply to slow movement and to fast.

I say, therefore, that the moving thing in such movement, after the separation of the moving body from the first projector, is the moved thing itself, not through any power [impressed] in it, so that the moving thing and the moved thing are entirely indistinguishable. If it is said that the new effect has some cause, and local movement is a new effect, I say that local movement is not a new effect . . . because it is nothing else than that the moving body is in different parts of space, and not in any one part, since two contradictories [of being in two different parts at once] cannot be true. Although any one part of the space which the moving body traverses is new in relation to the moving body, in that it is now where it was not before, absolutely it is not new. . . . It would indeed be surprising if my hand were to cause some power in the stone merely through coming into contact with the stone by local movement.[5]

This passage illustrates the gulf between a definition of a physical concept and a physical explanation. Ockham's principle of economy reduced the meaning of local movement to whatever moves successively; applied to nature, however, it is physically vacuous, for in refusing to multiply unnecessary entities in order to define movement as a concept, Ockham also excluded those very notions of causes and forces, other than moving thing and initial mover, essential to explain movement mechanically. Movement for him thus remained at the level of a definition. Paradoxically, although breaking with Aristotle's conception of movement, Ockham's treatment of movement is the summation of Aristotle's own classificatory approach, which ends not in abstraction from the study of nature itself but from the concepts formed about nature. When dissociated also from mathematics it is without scientific application, which is why Ockham played no part in the scientific developments of the later Middle Ages. The principle of inertia, of which he was at one time seen as the precursor, could never have been developed merely from the negative notion—that movement is whatever is not at rest and moves by itself—because it is without physical import, however philosophically liberating. To arrive at any solution there must first be a problem; but when the definition is taken as the explanation of something's nature, there is nothing further to be explained. Ockham thus obviated, in his own mind, the very need to inquire further into what keeps something moving, which inertia, as impetus, was designed to answer. Nor in confining himself to its purely philosophical definition did he show any conception of movement as a measurable quality, evinced by Buridan and the Mertonians and Parisians, in whose calculations it was to be so fruitful a concept.

That brings us to the second example of the comparison between Ockham and them, exemplified generally in the Mertonians' approach and more particularly in Heytesbury's treatise mentioned before. Heytesbury wrote it in about 1335 as probably the first of the writings of the group of fellows of Merton who pursued those new scientific topics. The other most notable members were Richard Swineshead and John of Dumbleton who together with Heytesbury flourished at Oxford from the 1330s to the 1350s, and probably not beyond. Their common inspiration was the *Treatise on Proportions* of Thomas Bradwardine, himself a fellow of Merton from at least 1321 until the middle 1330s, published in 1328. Bradwardine can therefore be regarded as the founder of Mertonian school of calculators which is above all distinguished for its mathematical approach, as Buridan can of the Paris school a decade or so later.

The Mertonians' most important scientific contributions were probably to mechanics, which unlike their pure mathematics, whose subtlety and sophistication were not to be approached and surpassed until the nineteenth century, were of direct application to the activities of their sixteenth-century successors. These included a clear distinction between dynamics, as the causes of movement, and kinematics, as the effects of movement considered in space and time; a new conception of velocity through the notion of instantaneous velocity, which in turn led to the so-called Mertonian mean-speed law or theorem—that uniform acceleration in a given time is equal to the speed of acceleration at its middle instant; and finally the definition of uniform acceleration as movement in which there are equal increases in speed in any equal periods of time and conversely for unequal or, difform, acceleration. The mean-speed law in particular became of widespread influence both in the new mathematical graphical representations of Nicholas of Oresme and subsequently in a modified form in Galileo's account of the free fall of bodies.

Here again, Ockham has been seen as the first to distinguish between dynamics and kinematics in his resolution of the controversy between the Arabian philosophers Avempace and Averroës, and transmitted to the West, over whether the resistance of the medium or the space traversed was the appropriate mode of analyzing movement over a period of time. Ockham recognized the validity of both as corresponding to what he termed the different conditions of "being in motion" and "being moved." But of itself that, once again, is no more than a conceptual difference, which however significant, does not alone constitute the separate fields of kinematics or dynamics, any more than to recognize that apples fall from trees constitutes the law of gravity. For that, the definition or observation must be transposed into mechanical terms, capable of providing a framework of explanation with its own hypotheses or axioms capable of verification and compatible with other mechanical hypotheses and data. That is to say, to become more than a definition requires those very theoretical and mechanical elements which Ockham's definition did not provide or show any indication of providing.

Those elements came initially from Bradwardine in his *Treatise on Proportions*, working in the separate and as yet isolated tradition represented by Gerard of Brussels's *Book on Movement*, regarded as the first properly kinematic treatise in the West, and written between 1187 and 1260. Bradwardine's third and fourth chapters are devoted precisely and explicitly to dynamics—"the proportion of velocities in movement in relation to the forces of the movers and the things moved"—and kinematics—"the magnitudes of the thing moved and of the space traversed." That distinction was almost at once adopted by his Mertonian followers, who, like Swineshead, distinguished between movement in relation to cause (dynamics) and movement in relation to effect (kinematics). More specifically, Bradwardine reformulated Aristotle's law of movement as the proportion between velocity, power, and resistance mathematically, which although wrong, came to form the basis of all subsequent calculations until the sixteenth century.

In doing so, Bradwardine, starting from the Aristotelian principle that movement occurs only when force is greater than resistance, sought to show that force and resistance as the determinants of velocity are in some kind of ratio, rather than a simple arithmetical difference; and that this ratio is in turn geometrical and not arithmetical. Consequently, in his own words, "the velocity of motion follows from a geometrical proportion," namely, that to produce twice the velocity, the proportion of force to resistance must be squared, not doubled; and triple the velocity follows from cubing, not tripling, the proportion of force to resistance; and so on. Bradwardine's followers and successors extended this formula to every kind of movement, including alteration of quality, condensation, and rarefaction. It inaugurated a new phase not only in medieval dynamics but mechanics and mathematical physics generally.

The effect can be seen upon the Mertonians, among whom the method of proportions taken in conjunction with terminist logic became applied to a wide range of physical and logical problems. Their most striking feature, as that of the Paris school, is that they are almost entirely without empirical verification or application. It is that which accounts for the extreme abstractness and sophistication of much of their logico-mathematical analysis, which did not become important for mathematics until the nineteenth century, with the development of a real number system. It is also part of the legacy of Aristotle, who, though his conception of reality, unlike that of the Pythagoreans and Plato, was nonmathematical was at the same time heavily indebted to the axiomatic method of Euclidean geometry, while the very abstractness of his approach fostered the logical analytical tendencies which lent themselves to mathematicizing.

Most of that is in evidence in Heytesbury's *Rules*.[6] To begin with, the only two authorities he cited were Aristotle and Averroës, a reminder of the

6. For what follows see C. Wilson, *William of Heytesbury*.

distinction we suggested earlier in the chapter between taking Aristotle as the source of natural scientific knowledge and rejecting him in his non- or anti-Christian aspect. As to Heytesbury's own contribution, in kinematics he gave a clear definition of uniform acceleration already mentioned, and also one of the earliest statements of instantaneous velocity which is measured by the space which *would* be described by a point if it were allowed to move for a period of time at the same velocity which it had at a given instant—a good example of the hypothetical nature of the calculation. In addition, the *Rules* also contain the Mertonian mean-speed law which also appears in that form in Galileo's *Two New Sciences*.

Central to Heytesbury's treatise, as a work designed for students in logic, are the different modes of supposition which he applies equally to physical and to mathematical problems, in turn employing physics and mathematics in a kind of mathematical physics for the analysis of logical problems. The whole cast of Heytesbury's and the Mertonians' thinking is to multiply hypotheses in a most un-Ockhamist manner, which is closer to the style of Duns Scotus without Scotus's metaphysical proclivities. That complexity is accentuated in the—probably—subsequent treatises of Swineshead and Dumbleton, as the result of pursuing more and more closely the mathematical and logical facets of the problems under discussion.

In Heytesbury's first three predominantly logical chapters, he was concerned with the application of the rules drawn from terminist logic, particularly supposition of terms and the distinction—going back to Aristotle and also treated by Ockham in his *Sum of Logic*—between the composite and divided senses of propositions. The last three chapters are mainly a mathematical treatment of physical problems such as the intensification and remission of forms, and those connected with points, lines, surfaces, and instants.

The intensification and remission of forms, or how forms became more and less intense, as one of the most universally raised because of its application to created grace, had met with a wide range of responses by Heytesbury's time. The most common ontological explanation that he, together with many fourteenth-century thinkers, adopted was that intensification and remission occurred through the addition of the same or a contrary quality. Inquiry for Heytesbury and his Mertonian contemporaries centered instead upon the logical and physical aspects of the change: of how to describe a subject in which the intensity of the quality varies from one point to another and of then quantifying the variation. This led to measuring the latitude, or range, of degrees in which it could occur. The term latitude, together with longitude, went back a long way to the Greeks, but they were given a new meaning by the Mertonians and Parisians as a way of representing intensities quantitatively by reference to a fixed scale. A form was taken as any variable quantity or actuality; the latitude of intensity was its numerical value; its change could then be measured according to another variable, the extension or longitude as the distance or time or quantity of matter involved. The concept of latitude and longitude applied to change in forms thus rested on the assumption that in Heytesbury's words "any finite latitude [i.e., qualitative intensity] is a certain quality." With John of Dumbleton at Merton and above all Nicholas of Oresme at Paris, it was given geometrical expression by graphing, as we shall mention shortly.

Heytesbury, however, kept to the so-called "word-algebra" of Bradwardine's proportions, where letters were used for the variables. In his *Rules*, he sought to express mathematically all the conceivable ways in which change can be ascribed to a subject, for example, in the proposition "Every man who is white runs" the different conditions in which someone can be called "white." That involved, among other things, deciding the furthest degree of intensity of whiteness, where in a finite range or latitude the middle degree is the maximum that does not suffice to enable the subject to be called "white." Hence, any greater degree of intensity will suffice to do so. Heytesbury then applies these two conditions to an analysis of qualitative variation in which at the beginning of a particular hour Socrates's face is partly white and partly black; during the hour the black area of Socrates's face condenses to zero quantity and the whiteness of the white area decreases continuously in quantity. If at the end of the hour the intensity of the whiteness is greater than the medium degree in the range of whiteness, it follows that Socrates will become white, although his whiteness decreases continuously in intensity. Heytesbury applied similar considerations to determine the degree of velocity required to establish the statement "Someone is running."

Heytesbury thus took logic in a quite opposite direction from Ockham. Where Ockham was concerned to reduce real signification to individual import, Heytesbury, while accepting that the real world consists only of real, absolute, objects and that mathematical and physical terms like "point," "line," "surface," "instant," "time," and "motion" are only concepts, was concerned to carry them to the limits of conceptual possibility. He therefore multiplied distinctions and hypotheses where Ockham excluded whatever could not be shown to represent real existence. Heytesbury's justification was the same distinction that Ockham had made between customary usage and strict meaning, but while for Ockham that had been to counter the first by the second, for Heytesbury it provides his justification for pursuing the implications of a proposition as far as imagination will take it, limited only by logical contradiction. Here, then, we see the fusing of the logical criterion of contradiction, which had become so important in the fourteenth century, with an entirely conceptual, nonempirical approach to nature. Like so many of his contemporaries who were doing the same in philosophy and theology the distinction between "speaking logically" or "according to imagination" and "speaking physically" or "strictly" was not a license for skepticism, to doubt everything; but a recognition of the hypothetical nature of the discussion in order to explore its implications. In the case of the Mertonians these were the mathematical implications of what could be said about physical events. That is what distinguished them. Instead of leading them to mere speculation, as in theology and philosophy, it led them to calculation and a new exactness. Although neither empirically founded nor corroborated, their activities were nevertheless directed to actual existence as opposed to what might or could exist under a different order. Hence their *imaginabilia* were not conceptions of an alternative reality but hypothetical and logical ways of understanding the workings of the existing one mathematically and quantitatively.

It was in that way that Heytesbury also treated the questions of a first and last instant, as the temporal limits of a period of change, and a maximum and minimum. Both derived from Aristotle, and became, the first especially, among the most debated problems of the fourteenth century, lending themselves to the distinction between physical and mathematical consideration.

First and last instants raised the issue of intrinsic and extrinsic boundaries between different aggregates, whether periods of time or movement, which physically—or "naturally speaking"—were applied to the magnitudes of Aristotelian physics: lengths, velocities, weights, and so on. Mathematically—or "logically" or "sophistically"—speaking the distinctions involved the logical and mathematical analysis of aggregates, limits, and infinitesimals. Its intricacy, although having no immediate scientific import in the succeeding period, took such analysis virtually to its limits verbally. Thus, among his other conclusions, Heytesbury showed that two infinitesimals can be of a different order, exemplified in the different rates of acceleration of Socrates and Plato. For if Socrates's rate is constantly half that of Plato's, at each instant of his movement Socrates will be moved with half the velocity of Plato; and if it were a quarter of Plato's rate, Socrates would be moved with a quarter of Plato's velocity, and so on infinitely.

Maximum and minimum were concerned with establishing the limits to the range of a power, i.e., of the ability to see objects at fixed or varying distances or of the capacity to lift weights. That, too, involved analysis of a continuum, derived from Aristotle's discussion of it, and also the enumeration of hypothetical rules for the nature and power of resistance.

At roughly the same time as Heytesbury, Buridan was introducing a number of new distinctions between types of action and passion; but they still remained within the categories of Aristotle's natural philosophy and were of a nonmathematical kind. Heytesbury, however, took that mathematical step and departed from Aristotle's physical and qualitative formulations. Using the terminology of the new logic, he stated a set of rules for all imaginable cases of an agent acting upon an object, in order to set extremes to classes and aggregates. "Maximum" and "minimum" apply to any boundary demarcating quantitative or qualitative change, including "quickest" and "slowest," "strongest" and "weakest," "first" and "last," and all powers are active or passive defined purely quantitatively in terms of being able to accomplish or suffer less in virtue of being able to accomplish or suffer more: for example, if Socrates can lift one hundred pounds, he can lift twenty pounds, and his capacity to lift is an active power; and, conversely, if Plato can see a grain of millet at a distance of a mile, he will be able to see a church at the same distance. They can in turn be affirmative or negative. Heytesbury then enunciates the conditions for deciding between an upper (active) boundary and a lower (passive) boundary having first established—logically—that one or other must hold. These conditions are: that there is a range in which the power concerned can act or be acted upon and another in which neither can occur; that whichever it is, it cannot hold for infinite values because they have no limit; that the division should be capable of a continuous range of values from no power at all to its boundary beyond which it cannot be acted upon, as an active power must be able to achieve any less amount than its maximum, and conversely for a passive power. On the basis of these principles, which had to wait until the nineteenth century to become mathematically significant, Heytesbury was able to calculate the different possibilities.

Richard Swineshead, known as the "Calculator," also wrote a treatise on maximum and minimum, which shows close affinities with Heytesbury's; but he was exclusively concerned in it with resistance to an agent, which, starting from Bradwardine's fundamental principle that no action follows from an equality between agent and resistance, took quantitative analysis much further, including those distinctions mentioned between debilitable and indebilitable, finite and infinite, powers defined quantitatively.[7] Both thinkers, like John of Dumbleton, also treated rarefaction and condensation, where matter receives greater and smaller dimensions, as a quantitative problem, in contrast to thirteenth-century Aristotelians like Albert the Great and St. Thomas Aquinas. They did not, however, agree over the way the changes could be measured. Heytesbury, in seeking to determine the velocity of the change, held that it depended upon the proportion of quantity acquired by the original volume in equal time, so that if two bodies of unequal volume acquired equal quantities in equal time, the body which acquired proportionately the greater quantity would have rarefied more quickly. Swineshead and Dumbleton rejected Heytesbury's opinion, Dumbleton because the velocity depends upon the precise amount of quantity acquired in a given time, Swineshead on the grounds that there is a relative proportion between rarity, quantity of matter and magnitude. His is the clearest exposition here as elsewhere, in this case leading to four laws: if two bodies have equal mass (as the quantity of matter), the one which has the greater volume will have proportionately the greater rarity; if two bodies are equal in volume they have equal mass; if two bodies are unequal in volume and equally rare, the one that is greater than the other has proportionately

---

7. On Swineshead's discussion of quantity see J. A. Weisheipl, "The Concept of Matter in Fourteenth Century Science" in McMullin, *The Concept of Matter*, pp. 164–67.

greater mass, and the one which is more rare has less mass; and, finally, if they are equal in volume and unequal in rarity then the less rare has proportionately less mass. From that it can be seen that the mass of quantity of matter is not to be taken in itself but is measured from its magnitude and density combined. This represented a well-developed physical theory of matter far removed from the older conception of primary matter and the physical dimensions which belonged to quantity as a separate category. Ockham had merged quantity with substance or quality having extension, denying quantity any separate ontological identity, but, once again, that is as far as he had taken his analysis. The Mertonians, and Swineshead in particular, had multiplied the distinctions into those between quantity, volume, and density or rarity, giving an entirely new quantitative statement of physical change.

Similar considerations apply to the discussions of movement in its other main categories of place and quality, which in Mertonian style were interpreted in their quantitative meanings of quickness and slowness, uniformity or difformity as the ways in which its velocity may vary. Hence, as we have said before, their interest was kinematic rather than dynamic. As in their treatment of maxima and minima the discussion is preponderantly hypothetical and mathematical, with no attempt at verification.

Within the limits of this book it would be otiose to pursue their particular analyses further. The differences between Ockham's purely philosophical and classificatory definition of natural phenomena in terms of individual existence, and that of the quantitative definition and analysis by Heytesbury and the Mertonian tradition should be apparent. They were not only differences of approach but of method and conception, leading to fundamentally divergent activities. Ockham's, however much it could open new windows on to the world, was designed to establish that all physical existence is individual existence. His interest in the physical world was thus principally an ontological one with his discussion of physical phenomena subordinated to a philosophical, rather than a physical, end, of their nature rather than their behavior. The Mertonians, on the other hand, subordinated the nature of the real world to their calculations over its behavior. They began from the very imaginabilia and hypotheses that Ockham eschewed because they took as given what he devoted himself to proving. Where he never passed beyond a qualitative evaluation of the individual, and its properties and relations, as the measure of truth and of physically ascertainable knowledge, they were not for the most part dealing in terms of qualitatively definable physical wholes and relations, but with the quantitative measures by which physical activity could be described. That, in the absence of an empirical foundation, took them almost entirely into the realms of mathematics and hypothesis, and accounts for their comparatively small influence upon the new developments in mechanics of the later sixteenth and the seventeenth centuries. But it also shows that those developments meant forsaking the Aristotelian conception of nature through merely qualitative classifications. If the Mertonians and Parisians were at once too oblivious of actual physical existence and too sophisticated in their calculations about it for their successors, they nevertheless made the breach in the Aristotelian system through which the new developments were to come.

The other main directions in which fourteenth-century thinkers contributed to it may be briefly indicated mainly by reference to Nicholas Oresme. On the basis particularly of the developments of kinematics, projectile movement and intensification and remission of forms already mentioned, Nicholas of Oresme, the sun in Parisian firmament of which Buridan was the creator, above all gave them new mathematical expression in the 1350s. His most signal contribution was to bring to perfection the method of representing changes either in quality or movement geometrically by means of coordinate lines in graphs: the latitude, or range of degrees in which a quality was intensified, was represented by a vertical line, and its longitude, or extension, as the quantity of matter or time or space involved, was represented by a horizontal line. The intensity *(intensio)* could then be measured in relation to its extension *(extensio)*. In that way velocity, as the latitude or intensification of movement, could be plotted in relation to its longitude or extension, to measure either uniform or changing acceleration or retardation by making an angle with the horizontal to form either a rectangle or a triangle, with its duration represented by a curved line. Oresme also extended the method to include three dimensional coordinates a second horizontal line representing the physical extent of the moving body. He applied the method to a whole range of changes, including the Mertonian mean speed theorem. In his case as in theirs, his examples were all imaginary. Although Oresme did not invent either the classifications or the method—he was anticipated in it by Gio-vanni di Casali by at least two years in his treatise *On the Velocity of Alteration*, based on the Mertonians' calculations, published in 1346 at the latest—he developed it in the form in which it was in widespread use in the later fourteenth century, receiving final fruition with Galileo.[8]

Oresme was perhaps the single most original scientific mind of the Middle Ages, and the nearest to a genuinely scientific thinker—even if an exclusively theoretical one—in the sense of forming his hypotheses from what he took to be the data of physical phenomena without reference to nonphysical or cosmological criteria. If he was not the inventor or even the anticipator of analytical geometry, his mathematical originality extended as well to the idea of fractional powers. He also altered Buridan's theory of impetus, explaining it as arising from an initial acceleration and leading to further acceleration. In his own words: "I say that this is the cause of the acceleration of a heavy body in the end: because it is accelerated in the beginning, it acquires such an impetus and this impetus acts with it in moving, so that other things being equal it is faster." And "it is corrupted by the retardation of movement, because velocity or acceleration is required for its conservation."[9] Thus although not explaining exactly how the initial acceleration occurs, Oresme's interpretation departed from Buridan's ex-planation in associating impetus with acceleration, not merely velocity, and no longer treating it as a permanent quality. He later applied it to projectile motion where the impetus produced by the initial acceleration from the projector keeps it moving and accelerating until resistance finally weakens the impetus and causes deceleration. Characteristically, Oresme developed the implications of his theory in two original directions. The first was the supposition that if a body could fall to the center of the earth it would acquire an impetus that would carry it beyond the center, oscillating around it until brought to rest. The second and more significant is a correct account of acceleration where the velocity increases arithmetically in equal periods of time rather than as a proportion, which was the position of Buridan and of Albert of Saxony, Oresme's contemporary and a less original member of the same school.

8. Clagett, *The Science of Mechanics in the Middle Ages*, ch. 6.
9. Ibid., p. 552.

Among his other achievements, Oresme carried further than any other scholastic the mathematics of Bradwardine's theory of proportions; he also developed Buridan's view that since the observation of movement is relative to the position of the observer, all astronomical phenomena could be equally well accounted for by positing the earth's diurnal movement. Both thinkers argued for it as a persuasion—not a proof—on the grounds that God does not do in a more complex manner what can be done more simply, which would be the earth's, rather than the heavens', rotation. But while Buridan rejected the idea for empirical as well as scriptural reasons, Oresme confined himself to the latter even while distinguishing, like those before him and Galileo afterwards, between the common usage and strict meaning of the scriptures. Equally, however, he concluded that "One cannot demonstrate by any experience whatever that the heavens are moved with daily movement, because regardless of whether it has been posited that the heavens and not the earth are so moved or that the earth and not the heavens is moved, if an observer is in the heavens and he sees the earth clearly, it would seem to be moved; and if the observer were on the earth, the heavens would seem to be moved."[10] Unlike Buridan, Oresme's theory of impetus as not being a permanent quality could not account for the perpetual movement of the heavens; hence, he had as an explanation only the rather vague suggestion that their movement "is in accordance with the proportions which their motive powers have to their resistances."

Although Copernicus was to employ similar arguments against the daily rotation of the heavens, particularly the enormous velocity that would be required, as well as a state of rest being more appropriate to their greater nobility, too much should not be made of this questioning of the accepted geostatic system. Oresme was only saying in mechanical terms what was by then generally agreed, that what lies outside human experience cannot be demonstrated. But he lacked any alternative dynamics to explain planetary theory; and conversely, equally like the majority of his century he accepted that God could create a plurality of worlds without contradiction, although "in fact there never was nor will there be any but a single corporeal world." The invocation of God's power cannot, therefore, be said to have entered into Oresme's calculations, nor into those of the Mertonians or the other

10. Ibid., p. 606.

members of the Paris school. Not only was it scientifically vacuous to posit alternative or infinite worlds, but it was destructive of the very regularities for which these thinkers were searching. They based their hypotheses, as we have said, on the physical laws which they derived from the present order; its acceptance and—at least hypothetical—certainty thus formed their point of departure. Without it, their calculations would have been vain. Like all those involved in the study of natural phenomena they had to proceed on an assumption of determinism, at the terrestrial, if not the cosmological, level. Moreover, as the same example of Oresme shows, a Christian conception of the universe, far from liberating Christian thinkers from a closed universe, kept it firmly fixed to a geostatic center, to escape which needed more than scientific reasoning, or appeal to God's omnipotence, as Galileo was to discover. Hence, as we have said before, it was not at the macrocosmic level of the universe, in the cosmological theories about it, that the important changes occurred, but microcosmically in the interstices of Aristotle's explanations of physical phenomena.

In that connection, the main interest of Oresme's position just considered was not with his cosmological speculations which were marginal to his total scientific enterprise, but with the doctrine of the relativity of perceived movement. Here he went further than Buridan in suggesting a closed mechanical system bounded by the observer's experience of the events which come within his range. Thus, in the analogy common to both thinkers, to an observer on a ship moving very swiftly eastwards, who was unaware of the movement, if "he drew his hand downwards describing a straight line against the mast of the ship it would seem to him that his hand moved with rectlinear movement only"—whereas in fact it would also be moving horizontally eastward: a doctrine further developed by Bruno and Galileo.

Perhaps the best commentary on the achievement of these thinkers is to be seen in how much of their conceptions and vocabulary passed into the use of their sixteenth-century successors, above all Galileo: equal movement, uniform and difform movement, degree of velocity, intensity of velocity, the comparison of instantaneous velocity at the end of the first time period and second time period, the definitions of uniform acceleration, unequal movement, uniformly unequal movement, unequal unequal movement, intension and remission of forms, free fall of bodies, from the theorem of uniform acceleration to the explanation of which the latter was crucial. All these derived from the Mertonians and Oresme, as well as their methods of calculation, to form a part of Galileo's thinking. That he put them to a new use is only to show at once how far reaching they were and how far short they fell of the fundamental change which they presaged.

The strength and novelty that led to these developments in the fourteenth century was their emancipation from theological and metaphysical preconceptions and the substitution of a mathematical for a metaphysical and purely conceptual account of nature. It was still limited and it lacked the empirical basis which was the precondition of fundamental scientific transformation. But for the first time, by departing from the qualitative categories of Aristotle, the Mertonians and Oresme, in particular, reached the threshold of the new mechanics at once in their conception of instantaneous velocity and their treatment of velocity as a ratio between space and time, and more generally in the development of a mathematics of change applicable to all forms of movement, local, qualitative, quantitative, violent. If they were still more interested in the methods and formulations of problems rather than the actual phenomena they were designed to explain, they nevertheless helped to create the language in which subsequent empirical investigation was to proceed. That only with Kepler, Copernicus, and Galileo did it lead to the transformation of the Aristotelian universe is the measure of the distance still to be traveled at the end of the fourteenth century. The Mertonians, Buridan, and Oresme had taken scientific enquiry to the threshold of a new world which their successors had not the fiber to cross. To have done so would have meant renouncing the classificatory and quasi-observational approach which these fourteenth-century thinkers had brought to the furthest possible pitch, and for the first time integrating mathematics with physical investigation as Galileo and his confreres were to do. Instead, they remained bounded by the old world for another two and a half centuries, repeating the theorems and proofs of their fourteenth-century predecessors as the now-accepted modes of doing science. For none of them were mathematics yet, the language in which the book of nature was written. As in philosophy and theology, the new coexisted with the old in growing disequilibrium to the point of dissolving the old equilibrium without substituting a new one.

IV. The Spiritual World

The disequilibrium in the outlook of the later Middle Ages is epitomized in its spiritual life. From the beginning of the fourteenth century, if not before, there was an increasing heterogeneity in both religious theory and practice. It was characterized by the search for a direct rapport with God, either through mystical union with him in the soul or through direct contact with his word in the Bible as the source of revealed truth and the pattern for a Christian life. Together they became the dominant religious forces of the fourteenth and earlier fifteenth centuries, expressed in a diversity of ways, on the one hand in the striving for mystical experience and personal piety and, on the other in the advocacy and pursuit of apostolic first principles through the reformation of the church and religious life. Each presented a challenge to the very *raison d'être* of the church, the first indirectly by putting inner revelation or personal sanctity before or beyond the authority of the church; the second directly, by opposing Christ's words and deeds as revealed in the Bible to the words and deeds of the existing church in its laws and practices which were only of human origin. Out of them grew the gradual rejection of the church in its visible form as the one mediator between the individual and God, which was at the center of Luther's theology and had its outcome in the loss of the church's universality.

In the fourteenth and earlier fifteenth centuries, that point had not yet been reached, even in the doctrines of Wycliffe and the extreme Hussites, while it did not enter into the world of mysticism or personal piety. The advocates of reform always saw themselves as belonging to the apostolic church of earlier Christian tradition, however imperfectly represented or betrayed by its hierarchy; their aim was to restore it to that tradition not to redefine its sacramental role. From that aspect, renewal was still sought within the existing framework. That is where both these tendencies—quietist and activist—converged without fusing in a new theological conception of the church which was to come with the Reformation. Whether it concerned the individual soul or the corporate life of the church, they substituted a spiritual for a merely sacramental criterion of Christian discipleship; inner experience rather than outward observance, personal piety rather than office, were seen as the test of membership and authority within Christ's mystical body. The effect was to undermine the institutional forms of the church. As in philosophy, theology, and knowledge of nature, it represented a reinterpretation of first principles to make them internally consistent or to bring them into alignment with experience or knowledge. But that very process of reinterpretation tended to undermine the system it was designed to uphold, in the ways we have been considering in this book.

In the case of spiritual life, the mystic and the reformer, differently though they proceeded from one another and among themselves, as well as from the philosopher, theologian, and enquirer into nature, nevertheless between them weakened the very conception of the church as the separate corporation, with its own laws, hierarchy, and prerogatives, which it had become over the preceding three centuries. In itself the questioning or opposing of such a notion was nothing new; it merely expressed tendencies that went back to the eleventh century at least and were inherent in the tensions between the church's universal spiritual mission, as the communion of all believers of every sort and condition, and its temporal form as an institution which had increasingly taken on those very attributes of exclusiveness and worldliness it was supposed to hold in contempt, making its hierarchy appear as one more privileged power.

It was that discrepancy between precept and practice, or renunciation of the world and involvement in it, which early came under attack and led to the growing revulsion against the abuses of spiritual power by the later thirteenth century; it rendered the church vulnerable just because it was universally accepted as the spiritual, and intellectual, arbiter of society. The desire to restore it to that exclusively spiritual role, personified in the life of Christ and his disciples, was the continuing theme of religious reform from apostolic groups like the Waldensians and Arnoldists in the twelfth century to the Hussites in the fifteenth, as well as of the growing regiment of moralists and publicists and ecclesiastical reformers which began with St. Bernard and culminated in the constitutional and practical attempts to reform the church at the General Councils of Constance (1415–18) and Basel (1431–41). But awareness of the priority of the spiritual over the temporal in the pursuit of a truly Christian life was not confined to reformers or critics; it equally inspired the mystical search for God in the soul and personal communion with Christ, which could vary from individual ascesis to the formation of pious groups like Beguines and later in the fourteenth century the *Devotio Moderna;* and indeed was the foundation of one of the two major orders of friars, the Franciscans, through the revelation that came to St. Francis in a vision that he must follow Christ's life of mendicant poverty and preaching.

What is so striking about these different responses to the same desire for spiritual renewal is that they cut across the different divisions between reformer and heretic, mystic and ecclesiastic, to recur again and again between the twelfth and the fifteenth centuries. And what distinguishes the later Middle Ages spiritually is the pervasiveness of those responses in a growing recognition, implicit and explicit, that the existing balance of Christian life was wrong. The attempt to restore it carried those involved beyond the sacramental boundaries of the church in search of a spirituality that they could no longer find within the church or in the established religious orders. That was the new development. The failure of the later medieval church and its institutional forms was not in any sudden moral failing; those with which it was charged—simony, pluralism, immorality, greed, apostasy—were common to most of the Middle Ages. It was a spiritual failure to meet the demands of a new spirituality that could no longer be contained within the existing structure and was not permitted new outlets under the latter's aegis. The consequences were precisely either a turning away from the church in the proliferation of extraecclesiastical groups and individuals devoted to their own religious experiences, or the demand for the church's own spiritualization by restoring it to its apostolic purity.[1]

In the case of mysticism,[2] it was the most pervasive spiritual force of the fourteenth century. Much of it was histrionic and probably spurious and some of it, associated with the heresy of the Free Spirit, debased, and in the accounts of it, heretical. But whatever the quality or authenticity of its different forms and practitioners, they had in common as mystical experience the achievement of an immediate awareness of God's presence within the soul not as the blessed vision of the saved but as a momentary and ineffable sense of union with him. It could only be attained through first detaching the soul from all awareness of itself and other things. Hence it involved withdrawal from the world and self-oblivion in order to return to it transfigured.

Now it was the exclusively personal and ineffable nature of mysticism that made it the one form of religious experience equally open to the lay, the illiterate, and the theologically uninitiated. It was therefore correspondingly more heterogeneous, to be found by the end of the thirteenth century among the lay communities of the Beguines and the Beghards in Northern France, the Low Countries, and the Rhineland, the religious orders including both the Dominicans and the Franciscans, and by then a remarkable series of women mystics among whom the "nuptaul mysticism" of Mathilde of Magdeburg was particularly influential. That diversity was accentuated in the fourteenth century as mysticism became more widespread. Undoubtedly the single most important new element was the speculative mysticism which derived from Meister Eckhart (c. 1260–1327)[3] and came to be associated initially with the Rhineland and the Dominican houses in Germany, directly inspiring the new school of Rhineland mystics of whom Hunry Suso, John Tauler, and John Ruysbroeck were the outstanding

1. For a general account of these developments, see G. Leff, *Heresy in the Later Middle Ages*, 2 vols. (Manchester, 1967).

2. The best general treatment is in J. Leclercq, F. Vandenbroucke, and L. Bouyer, *La Spiritualité du Moyen Age* (Paris, 1960) and bibliography. A good brief introduction is provided by G. Sitwell, *Medieval Spiritual Writers* (London, 1961).

3. Discussed in G. Leff, *Heresy in the Later Middle Ages*, 1: 260–94. See in particular V. Lossky, *Théologie Negative et Connaissance de Dieu chez Maître Eckhart* (Paris, 1960) and J. Ancelet-Hustache, *Meister Eckhart and Rhineland Mysticism* (London, 1959).

representatives. But beyond that, Eckhart indirectly helped to give a new impetus to popular and unofficial piety which extended over the greater part of the Rhineland, Low Countries, and Central Europe during the fourteenth century. There was also a resonance between a number of Eckhart's propositions extracted from his works and censured by a papal commission at Avignon in 1329 and the heresy of the Free Spirit. But, as in the similar censure of Ockham's opinions two years previously, when taken in isolation, they were made to sound far more extreme and unorthodox than in their proper context. Nevertheless, it was in something less than that context that his ideas spread; for beyond their precise exposition in his Latin theological writings, Eckhart was also one of the supreme preachers of his age at a time when preaching was regarded as indispensable to a religious vocation. There can be little doubt that it was through his sermons that Eckhart's outlook took its main hold; it was also through them, delivered in German to unsophisticated audiences of nuns and laymen, that it was distorted, partly through the necessarily simplified imagery which made his message so vivid, and partly through the almost inevitable garbling it received in being recorded and reported at second hand. It was there that his statements could sound pantheistic, above all his recurrent theme of the birth of the word—or God's son—in the soul. And it was precisely pantheism that was theologically the most dangerous accompaniment of Rhineland mysticism.

In a general sense that danger is inherent in any mysticism, since it can all too readily confuse the created with divine or oppose the divinity of inner revelation to that of revealed truth given in the Bible. But Eckhart's mysticism was particularly susceptible to such a construction because of the distinctive doctrine of the birth of the word in the soul. It derived from a fundamentally Neoplatonist conception of being and reality which came from the Dominican school at Cologne where he had studied and which also produced another outstanding mystic in his elder contemporary, Dietrich of Freiburg (d. 1310).

Eckhart's mysticism was conceived in terms of a metaphysics of essences as the source of all being and deriving from the archetypes in God's word (identified always with the Son as the second person of the Trinity). The soul for him was thus the object rather than the subject of this mystical theology, as the supreme and unique expression of the reuniting of a creature with its archetype in God. The whole cast of Eckhart's mysticism is speculative rather than affective, in the Western tradition; and it is one more paradox that this most complex of all forms of mysticism should have become the most popular, although henceforth always, even among his immediate and faithful disciples Suso and Tauler, detached from his metaphysics.

Eckhart's point of departure is in the two different ways God can be conceived: the first is in his own nature as pure being, when he is the One; he is then the hidden God, unknowable and indefinable save negatively as beyond all definition; the second is as creator when his nature can be differentiated as a Trinity and defined in relation to his creatures. By the first mode Eckhart follows the way of negative theology taken from the so-called pseudo-Denis or Dionysius (a fifth-century Greek Neoplatonist mistaken for St. Paul's disciple) of putting God above all names so that he cannot be simply called "being" or "wise" or "good" since these are merely created utterances drawn from finite beings. Hence everything affirmed of God must in turn be denied, to divest it of its created meaning, as the word "substance" applied to God must be negated of a subject because God can have no division in the manner of a created substance; and similarly with "being." The only term that can be unqualifiedly affirmed of God is "negation of the negation" which is reserved for God alone as the One, denoting being in its highest and fullest degree without limitation.

Considered as creator, however, the perpective changes. God is no longer undifferentiated being but a Trinity of persons through whose inner activity being is conferred on his creatures. Here the operative term applied to God is intellect, because it is through his son or the word as the source of all the archetypes of creatures that creation derives. Not that in God there is any real distinction between his being and intellect; they are, as Eckhart reiterates, inseparable with being the principle of intellect. It is rather that in the aspect of creator, God as intellect is primary, as at once the source of his creatures' origin and of the means by which they return to him as archetypes. That was Eckhart's gloss upon St. John's words that "In the beginning was the word" and at the end "All things were made by him." Taken in that sense, there is no contradiction as is sometimes suggested between the primacy of both being and intellect: one refers to God in himself; the other to him as creator. But they are each God himself; hence they imply no division within him.

The divine intellect, then, is what Eckhart describes as "the principle

of the whole of nature." The archetypes of all things which it contains
inhere in it virtually as the forms to which the species of things correspond;
but they only become actual outside God when they receive created being.
Accordingly, every creature is a compound of its uncreated essence or form
—man, lion, stone—which has its archetype in God, and of created being.
Thus, unlike God, whose being is his essence, it does not suffice to know
that a creature exists to know what it is; its nature remains independent
of its created existence, as justice and whiteness are both prior and subsequent to just men or white things. As forms they remain whole and undi-
vided in creatures, indifferent to the created things they inform. They
therefore can be discerned in separation from the latter; and it is to these
natures or essences, as opposed to things, that true knowledge belongs.

In the order of creation, however, being comes first, for it is the condition
for the actual existence of natures—as opposed to their virtual existence in
God's intellect—at all. Without being, the essences would remain uncreated. Hence such forms or essences have nothing to do with being but
only with natures and their intelligibility. Eckhart therefore made a radical
separation between a thing's creatability as being, which was entirely from
God, and its nature, which without being would be uncreated. It is therefore being that is common to everything created, and form which individu-
ates being into this identifiable thing, as a man or stone or fire. Thus being
and essence were for Eckhart, in contrast to virtually every Christian
thinker, ontologically distinct, as created and uncreated, within the same
structure of created being. In that dualism Eckhart stood alone and closer
to Plotinus with whom he also differentiated God from creatures as the
One from the many: the One as pure affirmation, the negation of all
nonbeing; the many as the negation of full being and of itself nonbeing.
The division between them was mediated by the uncreated essences in
God's intellect as the forms in which he conferred being where otherwise
there was none. Essences were thus the means of creatures' participation
in God's being; and to turn from created being to its uncreated essences
was a step along the path back to God. But no more than a step.

It is there that mystical exploration must begin; for with the way to God
barred by the limits of negation it could only be overcome by turning away
from the outward signs derived from being to the soul's own essence as the
sign of God. As God's intellect is the universal cause of being, so man's

intellect must go beyond being to God: they meet only as intelligences, not being. Now man's intellect comes first among his faculties, formed in the image of God; but like every essence its true nature is in its nonbeing; it has therefore to renounce its being in order to realize its uncreated nature. That involves entering the incorporeal and eternal region in the recesses of the soul variously named by Eckhart its ground or summit. There God resides as the spark or power or "something": like God, it is unnameable and indefinable. In reaching it, the soul is reunited with God in an ineffable communion. It is that which Eckhart calls the birth of the word in the soul.

It was its hypostatic nature that distinguished Eckhart's mysticism. The spark or power or something was an image of God himself as opposed to a faculty of the soul. Hence it was uncreated, belonging to not the soul but to God. As Eckhart said—for which he was to be censured in 1329—had the spark been the same as the soul, which he hastened to add it was not, the soul would itself have been uncreated. In fact, the spark was to be compared to the uncreated light in angels enabling them to seize God directly. It thereby radiated God's image as he was himself; it was thus not part of the soul, but what Eckhart termed its "life of reason" through which man became God's son. That, in effect, was to make the divine spark man's uncreated essence; it remained distinct from his created being like any other essence. But whereas justice or whiteness were known by abstracting their concepts from individual things, to find the divine spark in the soul meant renouncing all concepts. The man who did so became God's adopted son in being reunited with the word in God and with his own uncreated essence as the image of God.

Eckhart in the Neoplatonist tradition thus saw in the intellect man's image of God and the source of his deiformity, where the Augustinian tradition saw the will as the faculty of blessedness, a view then being reaffirmed by Duns Scotus. But Eckhart, although repeatedly emphasizing reason's greater nobility, went further than either tradition in his insistence that both will and intellect must be renounced in order to reach the spark in the soul. Self-oblivion was the condition of mystical awareness.

That was the other facet of Eckhart's mysticism. In contradistinction to the affective mysticism that became so prevalent in the later fourteenth century, to Eckhart awareness of self of any kind was to be rejected; even the recoil of sadness following the moment of ecstasy. Sadness was the accompaniment of outer things, in which there could be no consolation; it was a sign of man's involvement with the created, and so his separateness from God. Man in entering the ground of the soul entered into an eternal stillness, outside time, place, or movement. For that he had to detach himself from all physical desires and lose his identity as a finite being. To see God he must first cease to feel and see as a creature; only then could he pass beyond both corporeal and spiritual knowledge to complete inner awareness which came not from him but from the eternal uncreated light in the soul.

Eckhart's message, delivered in sermons as well as in mystical treatises written in German, was thus a recurrent call to empty the soul in order to let God enter and the son be born within it. That need for renunciation or poverty of spirit or detachment (the title of one of his German works) took precedence over everything else. Man must cease to exist as a creature, in his nothingness as a finite being, in order to reach nonexistence within God's being. That was the paradox which made Eckhart so liable to misconstruction: nonbeing as a creature was the condition of infinite and eternal being in God. It helps to explain Eckhart's apparent pantheistic tendencies and his depreciation of outward and sacramental forms: detachment came before all the virtues because it released man from created things and enabled him to achieve oneness with God; detachment meant that God loved the soul: it brought the soul so near to nothing that only God could enter. It was therefore above all other virtues just as it was above good works, fasting and prayer, all of which God would reward but which of themselves were inadequate to bring the soul to God. For oblivion is the end of detachment; and once reached, God draws the detached soul into himself: in becoming negated the soul becomes one with God. The detached soul cannot therefore feel humility or mercy, for they concern creatures, where it is free from created things and feelings. Nor can it pray because that is to ask something of God, but he who has renounced all things begs for nothing.

Detachment, then, in the loss of the soul's identity, became with Eckhart the focus of mystical activity and the central theme of later medieval mysticism. It was there that it departed from previous mystical tradition, where in the imagery of St. Bernard—more than anyone its founder—love was the bridegroom of the soul leading the created will to God's will in a divine embrace. The only image for Eckhart and his successors was the image of God in a soul emptied of all other images in the reaches beyond its own faculties.

The overwhelming tendency of Eckhart's mysticism was thus to make emptiness, not a supernatural access of love, the condition of spiritual attainment. Although Eckhart himself did on occasions suggest that grace provided the initial impulse to detachment, his emphasis, and much more that of his extreme followers, was upon the cessation of all feelings and strivings within the soul. It was precisely there that the Neoplatonist element of negation and passivity was hardest to reconcile with the Western emphasis upon the supernaturalizing activity of grace. To make renunciation rather than supernaturally infused love the agent leading the soul to God was to risk the very charges of pantheism and self-deification brought against Eckhart and subsequently identified with the heresy of the Free Spirit.

It was their very awareness of those dangers, expressed in their hostility to the Free Spirit, that helped Eckhart's followers, Tauler, Suso, and Ruysbroeck, to steer his mysticism away from its founder's metaphysical speculations into practical and devotional channels, in which form it was the most powerful influence in the spirituality of the later Middle Ages. For each of them the pursuit of detachment was the center of spiritual life leading to the rebirth of the son in the soul; but it could occur only through inner spiritual poverty by renouncing all desire and all images both of the senses and the intellect. It was that renunciation where nothing of self remained which they, particularly Suso and Ruysbroeck, expressly opposed to the false claims of the Free Spirit who took inner emptiness for deification and with it liberation from all external constraints. Not only, replied Suso, was a creature never completely annihilated as a creature so that he could become God, but it was in no longer seeking anything for itself that a soul was freed from itself and for God. Ruysbroeck probably went furthest in uniting detachment with grace. Tauler had treated the birth of the word in the soul as the third of its births, the first being in the eternal generation of the Son in God, and the second Christ's incarnation in the world. Both Tauler and Suso had emphasized the entirely passive nature of detachment, Suso making acceptance of suffering the beginning of detachment. Ruysbroeck employed more traditional elements in distinguishing a threefold unity in man: as an individual physical being, as a rational being, and as an essential nature in God without which he would be nothing. These correspond to the three levels of existence, in the active life, the life of yearning, and the contemplative life, each with its own perfection: the first of exterior exercises of piety and moral endeavor; the second, the three supernatural virtues of faith, hope and charity; the third, beyond ordinary comprehension present within the soul, but unrecognized, as sanctifying grace. To it belongs what Ruysbroeck calls union with God without means, whether external or internal in the seven gifts of the Holy Spirit, which inform the first two states of life. Although the third state of contemplative life begins in the second one with the gift of wisdom, it only reaches consummation when it becomes independent of reason in contemplation proper. It is then that the word is born in the soul and the soul returns to its essence in the divine idea of it in God's essence. It is thus reunited with God in ceasing to exist in itself.

The same emphasis upon renunciation is to be found in three of the four main English mystics of the same period, Richard Rolle, Walter Hilton, and the author of the *Cloud of Unknowing;* but only the last-named expresses it in similar Neoplatonic terms to the Rhineland mystics. The cloud of unknowing between the soul and God must be pierced by a cloud of forgetting in which all created images are banished in concentration upon the simplest idea of God. But here, even more than with the German mystics, Eckhart's severely Dionysian negative theology was being modified to permit that image of God to be identified with love, while, like Ruysbroeck, the anonymous author treats the gifts of the Holy Spirit, above all humility and charity, as steps on the way to contemplation. Much of what he and the other English mystics wrote was of a similarly practical and instructional nature.

It is that aspect which becomes increasingly prominent by the later fourteenth century. It was fostered by the very doctrine of detachment which, in depriving the soul of any images of its own, left it with only its own spiritual state. But there was also the cult of Christ's humanity as the object of the soul's love, originally made the object of mystical experience by St. Bernard. It was too deep-rooted to be confined to a mere hypostasis, as the birth of the word in the soul. For Julian of Norwich, the fourth English mystic, Christ was at the center of her mystical experience, while the reinstatement of grace by Eckhart's successors once again associated union of God directly with love of God. Hence the nonaffective, nonvolitional elements that Eckhart had abandoned had returned in full array within another fifty years, at the same time separated from the speculative and metaphysical framework in which Eckhart's mystical theology had been formed.

The *Devotio Moderna* most widely represented this new attitude, enshrined in the foremost devotional work of the fifteenth century, *The Imitation of Christ.* Gerard Groot (1340–84), the founder of the community of the Brethren of the Common Life at Deventer from which the New Devotion sprang in the 1370s, was personally influenced by Ruysbroeck, then prior of the Augustinian monastery of Groenendaal. Not by Ruysbroeck's Eckhartian doctrines of the soul but in the advice Groot received for following a life of practical devotion and spirituality. Harnessed to Groot's own desire for inner asceticism it led to the negative path of inner renunciation of self-will and outer renunciation of the temptations of the world, in the pursuit of a pure Christian life devoted to God. That was one stream —the popular and nonheretical one—in which Eckhartian mysticism issued.

The other stream was a new intellectual emphasis which appeared at the end of the fourteenth century and the beginning of the fifteenth, notably with John Gerson (1363–1429), chancellor of Paris university and a leading figure at the Council of Constance (1414–18). That, too, marks a return to an earlier tradition, partly deriving from St. Bonaventure (1224–74) where a higher intellect, or simple intelligence, leading to contemplation, and a higher appetite in the will, or synderesis, leading to ecstasy, together combine to unite the soul to God in a complete union of love. Gerson was among the fiercest opponents of the heresy of the Free Spirit, repeatedly attacking them in work after work for their pretense of loving God, in the name of which they defiled him, and their pantheism; for the latter he also criticized Ruysbroeck in a series of letters even while commending Ruysbroeck's own exposure of the Free Spirit. To Gerson, uncontrolled mystical experience, without theological understanding, was among the greatest perils of the time. His own emphasis upon meditative prayer, recalling the prescholastic monastic tradition, was in reaction to the proliferation of pseudomysticism; he accompanied it with the need to have a sense of vocation for a contemplative life. In both these respects Gerson marks the parting of the ways for medieval mysticism, turning aside from it as a form of personal spirituality open to anyone without prior instruction or self-examination. Conversely, mysticism in its popular form had largely become a moral and practical spirituality either, with the Brethren of the Common Life or the different Beguine communities, practiced as an independent way of life, or, among the Lollards and the Hussites, as a more militant demand for the church to renounce the evils of the world and reform itself. In each case it represented a spectrum of views and practices. What they had in common was the desire for direct encounter with God, either within the soul, in withdrawal from the world, or in making the world—or rather its spiritual part—conform to Christ's own life in the world. In both aspects the image of Christ was the focus of activity as it was in so much else of the religious life of the period. How it affected the attitude to the church as an institution we must now finally consider.

Of the new developments which we have been examining in this book, none is more striking than the emergence of a new critical attitude to the church conceived in terms of an historical interpretation of it.[4] How genuinely historical is secondary to the then prevailing belief in its historicity. Once again it concerned Christ as a man; but this time as an historical figure in his life on earth, which, together with that of his disciples, was taken as the model of the apostolic church. As the ideal of what the original church had been, it came by the later thirteenth century increasingly to be regarded as the norm of what the church must always be and opposed to what it had by then become.

The notion of an apostolic ideal, founded upon the testimony of the Bible, thus introduced a discontinuity between an apostolic and a post-apostolic—indeed nonapostolic—church. From the time of Dante (1265–1321) it became one of the greatest challenges to the later medieval church

4. The remainder of this chapter is a development of what I have written in *Heresy in the Later Middle Ages*, especially chs. 1, 2, 5, 6, and 7; "The Apostolic Ideal in Later Medieval Ecclesiology," *Journal of Theological Studies* N.S. 17 (1967): 58–82; "John Wyclif: The Path to Dissent," *Proceedings of the British Academy* 52 (1966): 143–80; "The Making of the Myth of a True Church in the Later Middle Ages," *The Journal of Medieval and Renaissance Studies* 1 (1971): 1–15; and more recently *William of Ockham* (Manchester, 1975), ch. 10. Documentation is provided there, to which can be added A. S. McGrade, *The Political Thought of William of Ockham* (Cambridge, 1974).

in its existing state and to the temporal ramifications of ecclesiastical power expressed in the doctrine of a papal plenitude of power. The apostolic ideal influenced not only thinkers and publicists as diverse as Dante, Marsilius of Padua, William of Ockham, Dietrich of Niem, Wycliffe and Hus, but also entered into popular and religious belief, among the Waldensians and Franciscan Spirituals and later the English Lollards and the Hussites. For all of them in different ways it represented a standard of opposition to the present church, and a justification for its reform. As such it engendered a new critical attitude not only to the church as an institution but to the very nature of a Christian society.

To begin with, the appeal to an original past made the concept of the church historical rather than abstract. Instead of having existed the same for all time, it had undergone different phases of development, until it had reached its present one of decline. That in turn was the result of certain historical events, widely associated with the so-called Donation of Constantine—an eighth-century forgery but until the later fifteenth century generally accepted as authentic—by which the Emperor Constantine made over the Western lands of the Roman Empire to the jurisdiction of the pope. But however it occurred, the break with the apostolic church came through the introduction of wealth and power into the body of Christ. From that had flowed all the subsequent evils which had reached their culmination in the present, i.e., later thirteenth and fourteenth centuries, of a church with lust for possessions and money, legal rights, and absolute power extending over temporal rulers.

Such a conception also meant a break with the Augustinian conception of the militant church as the visible expression of God's saving will on earth. For it was precisely in its visible form as a privileged corporate hierarchy that it was no longer to be equated with the unfolding of God's providential design. Rather, its failings were to be interpreted as a falling away from Christ which could only be remedied by restoring the church to the pattern of his life.

That in the second place made Christ not only head of the church in his divinity but judge of the visible church in his humanity. It is perhaps the supreme paradox that in the criticism of the later medieval church, the figure of Christ as a man became the main threat to the divinity of the church as an institution. The events of his life on earth were made the touchstone of ecclesiastical practice. Christ and the apostles, possessionless and humble, meant a church without dominion or jurisdiction. The church as a Christ's body could not be a privileged corporation; its only identity was the spiritual communion of all believers in Christ. To follow Christ's example of renunciation of the world was thus the true test of discipleship and incumbent upon all those who as priests claimed to exercise his sacramental authority.

This ideal thus came from treating Christ as an historical figure, as a man who had lived among other men. He was no less divine for having done so; on the contrary, as God's son, his human existence had provided the divinely ordained norm for all men. That is what made it so destructive of the authority of the existing church, for it was an entirely different norm from the latter's: of poverty, humility, and spiritual ministration, with no other power than that which came through charity and God's word. However idealized, as applied to the early church as an historical reality, it nevertheless owed its force to treating what was contained in the Bible as historical fact.

That is the third element in the emergence of an apostolic ideal. The Bible was at once its foundation and its justification, for, in being interpreted historically, Christ's words and deeds were taken for real historical events to the point where they became a challenge to the life and practices of the present church. That gave a new role to the Bible, not only as the main source of criticism of contemporary spiritual life but at the expense of all other forms of canonical truth, above all what were regarded as the purely human ordinances of canon law. The exalting of scriptural truth culminated in Wycliffe and the Hussite Brotherhoods, in their exclusion of all that was nonscriptural. But there was not at any time in the later Middle Ages a doctrine of *scriptura sola;* the very appeal for a return to Christ's example was also for a return to the tradition of his apostolic church. They were not conceived as distinct; for the attack was not upon tradition itself but departure from a tradition redefined as apostolic. That was the novelty. Since the Bible was the testimony of what that tradition should be, the effect was to make the Bible not merely the spiritual but also the institutional arbiter of the church. By the fourteenth century, for the first time the existing church was being seriously questioned as an institution, or more exactly in its postapostolic institutional form, and not simply

for the moral failings of its personnel. There were two far-reaching consequences.

The first was that, in having a past, the church also had a future. And
that future was to return it to its past. Such a notion had gradually evolved
during the thirteenth century in the various apocalyptic groups, above all
the Franciscan Spirituals influenced by the prophecies of Joachim of Fiore
(c. 1145–1202) of a coming third age of spiritual renewal. Although by the
later thirteenth century this belief had taken an extreme form that went
far beyond the teachings of Joachim himself, its inspiration was the expec-
tation of the imminent coming of a new spiritual third age of gold which
would transform the church and the whole world. It was based precisely
upon an historical interpretation of the Bible, which however figurative,
conceived its two testaments as Christian history divided into different
epochs and phases. Its periodizing went back to St. Augustine's division of
Christian history into seven ages; and Joachim's scheme was only one of
a number during the twelfth century when the writing of universal history
became an established genre. Nevertheless, it was his that took hold; his
teachings on the coming of a new order of spiritual monks, who would
renew the church in the sixth and penultimate period of the second age
before its transformation in a final third age, offered a parallel to the new
mendicant orders of Franciscans and Dominicans, dedicated to poverty and
preaching, upon which members of both orders seized. Among the extreme
wing of the Franciscans, dedicated to absolute poverty, that ideal was fused
with Joachist prophecy. Observance of evangelical poverty became the
touchstone of loyalty to Christ and the badge of the renewers of his life
—as the one true spiritual church—in the new age to come. While not
elaborated into a concept of an apostolic church—neither Joachim nor the
Franciscan Spirituals took the Donation of Constantine as the source of all
evil and Joachim praised Constantine for recognizing the church—poverty
together with the other evangelical virtues of humility and submission
inseparable from it, became the model for the future church, and was given
divine import. Correspondingly, its denial was the mark of antichrist.

The prevalance of an apocalyptic outlook is to be found throughout the
fourteenth century, not always in a Joachimist form, but in the sense of
impending dissolution and transformation associated particularly with the
need to restore Christ's apostolic simplicity: in Dante; the line of pre-

Hussite and Hussite preachers and reformers, beginning with Conrad of Waldhausen in the 1360s, and their corresponding sects; in the various dissident Franciscan groups and their lay followers, including Cola di Rienzo at Rome in the later 1340s and 1350s; and in different—nonapostolic—forms by thinkers like Gerson or in the mystical and prophetic experiences of Catherine of Siena, as well as in the bands of Flagellants stimulated by the horror of the Black Death between 1348 and 1350 and subsequent epidemics of Plague. The outbreak of the Great Schism within the papacy from 1378 to 1417 only helped to stimulate—as in Wycliffe and the Hussites—the sense of impending cataclysm.

Parallel to this widely diffused apocalyptic sense was an equally strongly imbued apostolic sense of mission among the Waldensians; only with them it was not apocalyptic. They, too, represented a form of piety derived from veneration of the Bible as the direct source of truth and the desire to respond to the message which they found in it, namely, to emulate Christ's life on earth. They had originated as one of a number of apostolic reforming groups in the twelfth century, in about 1176, in circumstances not dissimilar from those in which the Franciscans originated. But they had from the outset been a lay movement, and it was for overstepping the limits imposed by the church upon their preaching and spiritual activities that led within a few years to their excommunication. Henceforth they increasingly framed their beliefs as a direct counterclaim to the authority of the Roman church. They affirmed they had become the one true church since the defection of the church of Rome when it accepted Constantine's donation. Henceforth the Roman church was the church of the wicked; through its betrayal of Christ, it had lost its sacramental powers which had passed to the "perfect"—or ministers—of the Waldensian church. In contrast to the hierarchy of the Roman church, they were distinguished by their life of physical austerity and spiritual ministration. The doctrine of the Donation of Constantine thus acted as the historical justification for the Waldensians' denial of the laws and practices of the Roman church. Beyond the refusal to accept the ministrations of its priests and hierarchy, for being in mortal sin as members of the church of the damned, their rejection included virtually the whole of the church's ritual: saints' days, feast days, fast days, vigils, pilgrimages, offices, benedictions, all prayers except the Lord's Prayer, all forms of coercion, the passing of judgments, the taking of oaths, the use of material elements, like oil and water, in the sacraments, as well as their number, the belief in purgatory which rendered prayers for the dead or the intercession of the saints otiose. Even churches were at best merely stone buildings, and cemeteries pieces of open ground.

How much the prevalence of these ideas in the later Middle Ages, including their conception of the Donation of Constantine, owed to the Waldensians cannot be said. But as coming nearest to an alternative church during the Middle Ages, which, with its own congregations and hierarchy diffused over Northern Italy and most of Central Europe by the end of the thirteenth century, survived the Middle Ages, it was representative of a widespread reforming spirituality shared among others with the English Lollards and Hussites and expressed by the individuals we have mentioned. It derived from the belief in an original apostolic church which had been betrayed by the pope, Sylvester I, who had accepted Constantine's gift, and his successors who had not renounced it. What distinguished the true church of Christ was precisely the renunciation of the world that had been brought into the church with that gift. The test of its membership was the very spiritual probity, in austerity of life and simplicity of belief, based upon the Bible as the law of conduct, which the Roman church had irretrievably lost. These were the qualities which were to be opposed to the dead weight of postapostolic tradition in all its ramifications—its elaborate hierarchy, decretals, enactments of synods, material wealth, and corporate privilege, which rendered null and void its sacramental authority. In their stead was the direct mediation of God's word and the emulation of Christ. The Christian believer in opposing the present church, therefore, even to the point of rejecting the ministrations of the priesthood, was on that view only becoming a thoroughgoing apostle of Christ; he was bringing Christian practice into conformity with Christian precept. For that, only obedience to Christ was required.

That brings us to the second consequence, and perhaps the most universal of the new attitudes to the church in the fourteenth century: the breaking down of a purely institutional conception of the church defined in terms of the juridical and canonical authority of its hierarchy, and the substitution instead of faith in Christ through participation in his word and life as contained in the Bible. The distinction between those in orders and laymen was secondary or irrelevant or even—for the Waldensians, Hussites, and Wycliffe, and, in a modified form, Ockham—misleading. Far from spiritual office sanctifying its holder, it provided no guarantee that he who held it was fitted to exercise it. Sanctity was from God's grace, conferred by him alone and equally accessible to laymen. The one condition was faith; and the only test of faith was conformity to Christ's law given in the Bible. Not only therefore did the authority of the church not exclusively reside in its hierarchy, but the failure to live according to Christ could mean the deposition of any or all of its members, from the pope downward, and their supersession precisely at the hands of faithful laymen as equally of the body of Christ. This attitude was crystallized in the development of conciliar theory in the later fourteenth and earlier fifteenth centuries to overcome the Great Schism. In order to do so, the principle was affirmed that a General Council representing all the faithful and if necessary summoned or presided over by a layman could depose an erring pope—or in this case, three popes. At Constance in 1415 under the auspices of the Emperor, that was achieved. Although neither in theory nor in practice having anything in common with a nonhierarchial conception of the church, and on the way burning Hus for denying the sacrosanctity of the pope, the General Council of Constance, and even more but less efficaciously that of Basel, came as near as any events in the Middle Ages to accepting a wider and less exclusive definition of the church. In that they were expressing, albeit in a muffled and ultimately ineffectual way, the need for reform.

How widely the awareness of that need came in the fourteenth century to be conceived in noninstitutional, nonhierarchical terms can be seen from the diversity of standpoints from which it was held, quite apart from the popular apocalyptic and reforming groups already mentioned. Indeed, it is the convergence between these different levels in certain common attitudes towards the church, and the criteria for spiritual life, that is so striking.

Among the most prominent examples we may mention first, in order of appearance, Dante's conception of the church which was among the earliest nonsectarian statements of the apostolic ideal. Like the empire, the church was of divine origin, coming from Christ and his apostles; and just as it was the task of the emperor to restore the unity of mankind, so it was incumbent upon Christ's successors to be true to his apostolic life. Failure in each case disqualified them: as Albert of Austria, Henry VII's successor as emperor, became a mere German for deserting his mission to regain the empire, so such popes as Nicholas III, Boniface VIII, and Clement V would be in the eighth circle of hell as punishment for simony. The form of the church was "nothing else than the life of Christ." It should therefore have no possessions and no coercive power. For that reason Dante rejected the Donation of Constantine. It was given neither to emperors to alienate their dominions nor to popes to rule over them. In having done so, claiming temporal powers that did not belong to them and spiritual powers reserved to Christ alone, the Donation had been the beginning of the church's ills. For a time Christ's spirit had been renewed by the coming of the Dominican and Franciscan orders. Although not a Franciscan or a Joachimist, Dante seems to have been powerfully influenced by both. In the *Paradiso*, first through St. Thomas Aquinas and next St. Bonaventure, he extols poverty and then condemns the falling away from it in their two orders. He praises Joachim of Fiore as a true prophet, and describes St. Dominic and St. Francis, in reminiscent terms, as the renewers of Christ's life and teachings. His attack upon the departure of the church from its apostolic principles culminates in St. Peter's denunciation of Boniface VIII who has disqualified himself as pope by his betrayal of the church. By the time of the *Paradiso*, Dante had ceased to look for human intervention to restore it, which perhaps made his bitterness at its decline within his own lifetime all the greater.

But where Dante looked to Providence, which "will swift lend aid," for remedy, others such as Marsilius of Padua (c. 1275–1343) sought it in lay intervention. Of all the new interpretations of the nature and role of spiritual authority, he transformed the attack upon its abuses and excessive claims, in the doctrine of the papal plenitude of power, to an attack upon the very foundations of an independent ecclesiastical and papal jurisdiction. Marsilius was the first theorist to deny the church its own autonomy as an institution.

He did so in the same belief as Dante in an original apostolic church which had constituted the primitive church from the time of its foundation by Christ until the Donation of Constantine. Like Dante and also Ockham, he opposed its biblical authority to the false pretensions of the canonists whom, like them, he detested. It is with Marsilius that the Bible is explicitly treated as an historical record of real events, supported by chronicle and other documentary evidence including, as he believed, that of the Donation of Constantine together with the interpretations of the church fathers and other canonical authorities. What Marsilius deduced from all these was that Christ and the disciples had lived in poverty, simplicity, and equality. Christ had come into the world to exercise spiritual not temporal authority. He had declared before Pilate that his kingdom was not of this world, and throughout his life in it he had always rendered unto Caesar. As Christ had submitted, so must the church. Moreover, in the early church there had been no hierarchy based upon the coercive jurisdiction of bishops and popes; only the two orders of priest and deacon.

That was the second feature of Marsilius's attack and with Wycliffe a direct challenge to ecclesiastical authority: from it he concluded, again on the basis of scriptural evidence, or lack of it, that there was no papal primacy by which the pope was head of the church. First, because Peter's position as foremost among the apostles had been personal to him. Second, that primacy had never been passed on to the pope as Peter's successor and Christ's vicar: any bishop was equally the apostles' successor and had his power immediately confirmed by Christ on condition that he conformed to the apostolic life. Third, there was only one head of the church and that was Christ; the bishop of Rome, on the other hand, had no authority outside his diocese, least of all headship over the whole church. Christ's commission to Peter in Matthew 16:18, giving him the keys of the church did not, as had been traditionally held, mean that Peter was the rock upon which the church was built. Only Christ could be that because he alone, as divine, was inerrable and impeccable. He had no need of a vicar. Finally, there was nothing to show historically that Peter had been bishop of Rome.

The papacy was thus a purely human institution; and Marsilius sought its origins historically in the desire of other churches to emulate the virtues of Peter and Paul. At first they had done so by submitting to Rome voluntarily; afterward submission had taken on the force of election. But it owed nothing to any words of Christ or the apostles. At the synod of Nicaea, the Emperor Constantine had confirmed the pope's primacy by decree, upon which succeeding popes had based their authority. Accordingly, the pope enjoyed no more power than any other bishop; for he was not God's vicegerent and he had no special spiritual prerogatives denied to the rest of the priesthood; all priests as the successors of the apostles had the power of the keys. The same lack of any special powers applied equally to the cardinals. Marsilius similarly attacked ecclesiastical possessions; they had come with the Donation of Constantine to which Marsilius attributed the church's decline. Loyalty to Christ meant renunciation of all property and rights of litigation.

To restore the church to Christ, Marsilius sought to minimize the differences between the priesthood as a distinct body and the rest of the faithful. That restricted it to an exclusively spiritual role, and its law to what was contained in the Bible. The church thereby lost all independent jurisdiction, including the power of excommunication, which like all matters of faith, in involving the whole community, must be decided by the community as a whole in a general council—a foreshadowing of later conciliar theory. In order to end the abuses of spiritual power, which had deformed the church and led to schism, Marsilius proposed that the church should be forcibly returned to its apostolic state of poverty and simplicity, by its submission in all things other than purely spiritual ministration, of the sacraments and worship, to the power of the temporal ruler. The effect of such a program would have dissolved the church as an independent corporation. Which was Marsilius's aim. Not surprisingly he was excommunicated for his views, written in his *Defender of the Peace*, in 1324; he sought refuge at the court of the pope's enemy, Ludwig of Bavaria, where Ockham also went in 1327.

Marsilius was echoed in his views, explicitly by Dietrich of Niem, who was never a heretic and took a leading part in the Council of Constance, and implicitly but more far-reachingly by John Wycliffe, condemned by the Council thirty years after his death in 1384. Both added their own distinction between a visible church in this world and the true church existing outside time and place. But whereas Dietrich sought only to reconcile them in overcoming present schism in the visible church, Wycliffe denied any necessary correspondence between them. For him, the true church consisted only of the saved. The damned were eternally excluded from it. Hence they formed two separate congregations: one under Christ, the other under Antichrist. What had previously been an eschatological division, of the separation of the two after this world, became for Wycliffe an eternal division. Since, moreover, no one knew whether he was damned or saved there was nothing to tell who was of the true church. Hence any priest or pope may not be a true priest or pope at all. At that metaphysical level of eternally distinct bodies, Wycliffe took the disjunction between office and membership further than anyone before him. He also gave an even more exalted role to the Bible every word of which—whether literally or otherwise—he believed was eternally true. His conception of both Bible and church was in keeping with his conviction that everything was in its essence—in God—timeless and unchanging. But while it led him to fundamentalism over the Bible, it caused his rejection of the existing visible church for its archetypal reality. The Bible as God's word was true in itself; it therefore literally sufficed. To seek the church in its archetypal reality meant going beyond its present earthly form to its true nature in God. That could only be known from the Bible as God's revelation. The effect of this combination was virtually to nullify the authority, and indeed, the existence, of the visible church.

In the first place, with the church exclusively of the elect, wherever they might be, it was no longer the congregation of all the faithful united by baptism. That meant that as a visible body it effectively lost any identity. Just as there could be no guarantee of the authority of any pope, prelate, or priest, so every member of the elect, as alone of the true church, could be directly ordained of God and receive from him sacerdotal powers. As Wycliffe expressed it, there was no need to be a cleric in orders to be a priest; and conversely, to be ordained a priest offered no certainty of God's authority or approval. Although Wycliffe never went to the point of openly rejecting the sacramental power of the hierarchy, or counseling refusal of the sacraments, the whole tendency of his outlook was to depreciate them and minimize the role of the priesthood. He repeatedly attacked the laws requiring annual communion and auricular confession; while at the same time he affirmed that the saved layman, whoever he might be, could hear confessions and give pardons as well as the pope.

Wycliffe did not stop there. He also—inconsistently with his own conception of the church as unknowable—employed the same doctrine of the apostolic ideal defined according to the Bible, as the only source and criterion of truth, to judge and condemn the existing church for failing to conform to Christ's evangelical life. Here he employed the full array of Marsilius's arguments to deny the primacy and, unlike Marsilius, also the legitimacy of the pope and cardinals. Thus fundamentalism was made to serve morality as well as metaphysics; their combination took him to a more extreme position than anyone else. He at once denied that a pope or priest could exercise his office, unless he had received a special revelation—an unverifiable requirement; and he used the Bible to discount most of the offices, other than of priest and deacon, and all the laws, jurisdictions, wealth, and "Caesarian" practices, such as excommunication, indulgences, and crusade, of the existing church, and damn those implicated in them as antichrist. By the time of his latest works, written in the last four years of his life, that condemnation had come to include virtually the whole of the visible church—the "Caesarian" clergy as he called them—as well as the religious orders or "sects"; they all bore the marks of antichrist, pride and avarice, in contrast to the poverty and humility which were the badge of Christ, extolled by Wycliffe with an almost Franciscan fervor.

Like Marsilius, he saw the source of these evils in the Donation of Constantine, which for him constituted the crime of secularization and led to papal usurpation of Christ's authority. It could only be expiated by desecularization, which for Wycliffe, even more explicitly than Marsilius, meant the wholesale expropriation of the church from all its lands, possessions, and jurisdiction by the king and the lay lords, thereby returning the priesthood to a life of preaching and spiritual ministration, living only on alms as the voluntary offerings of the faithful. Wycliffe, thus having divested the hierarchy of any inherent spiritual authority, reduced it to an exclusively noninstitutional form. With God the direct source of all spiritual power, and the Bible the sole repository of his word, there was no place for any mediator between either those who were eternally of the church or those eternally excluded from it.

Wycliffe together with Marsilius and Dietrich of Niem, carried frontal attack upon the existing church to the point where it lost any independent institutional identity. But he also went further in undermining the very justification for a visible church in face of the one true church outside time and space, which was eternally and exclusively of the elect who through God's grace of predestination could never, whatever their temporal vicissitudes, fail.

Ockham, in contrast, denied neither the church as an independent institution nor the indispensability of its mediation. But he did deny the necessity of the existing form of either; and in a manner more insidious and damaging than perhaps any other thinker. He did so from two aspects. The first was the apostolic ideal, which as a Franciscan he defended against John XXII in the pope's condemnation in 1323 of the doctrine of Christ's absolute poverty; the second was his conception of the universal church. Ockham interpreted the first in the slogan "Evangelical law is the law of liberty," by which he meant that through Christ's renunciation of all temporalities and jurisdiction his successors had no right to claim them. When they did so, as John XXII had done, they became heretics. Neither the pope nor any other ecclesiastic therefore could interfere with or impose his will upon either the faithful or infidels beyond what was requisite to fulfill Christ's precepts; everything else, including the supererogatory wishes of those following a religious vocation, like the Franciscans' vow of absolute poverty, or the temporal rights of rulers like the emperor, lay outside their authority. Evangelical liberty was thus "to be understood negatively, namely, that it introduced no heavy burden and that no one was made the slave of another, nor that only an exterior cult of God was imposed upon all Christians." It was Ockham's counter to the papal claim to an absolute plenitude of power, which involved just such impositions.

Gradually he extended it from a limitation upon the exercise of all spiritual power to the limitations of those exercising it. Here he said substantially what Marsilius had said and what Wycliffe was to say, without the secular implications of one or the metaphysical nuances of the other. Since Christ had abjured all wealth and power, when he had declared that his kingdom was not of this world and had rendered unto Caesar, how much more was the same life incumbent upon his successors who were only mortal men. A pope was only a man like any other, liable to sin and error; he could not work miracles, or rise from the dead, or institute new sacraments. Christ was free from sin and error, and he alone could do such things because he was God. Nor did office overcome its bearer's human limitations; it neither confers nor confirms, or increases, grace, but merely makes the lapse from grace greater the higher the office is. Consequently a pope can fall into heresy, which is just what John XXII had done first in attacking Franciscan poverty and then in his doctrine of the beatific vision. In reiterating that accusation of heresy in work after work, and extending it to John XXII's successors, Benedict XII and Clement VI, for not repudiating their predecessor's errors, Ockham more than anyone helped to bring into currency the accepted canonist doctrine that a pope who fell into error excludes himself from the church and so ceases to be pope. That notion was to have an important bearing upon the theory that a general council could depose a pope.

That brings us to the second aspect of Ockham's ecclesiology, his concept of the universal church. In contrast to the particular churches in the world, it alone is inerrable and infallible because it embraces all those believers, from its beginning in the time of the apostles to the present, who are united in the same faith and have not erred against it. For that reason the universal church can never fall away from Christ; it is at once greater than any individual church—Rome or Constantinople—in existing throughout time and beyond space, and it may in its visible form be less than any such congregation, since an entire church could defect through error. It is that which for Ockham prevents the hierarchy—or indeed the entire church in its present existence—from possessing those attributes which belong to the universal church alone, for the militant church can never be more than a part of the whole, which alone is universal. From that it follows in the second place that faith alone was the sole test of conformity with the universal church and so of legitimate ecclesiastical authority. That effectively destroyed the sacramental prerogative of the hierarchy as an order and substituted instead the universal prerogative of baptism. Not only could the pope or any part of the church—the whole college of cardinals, the hierarchy, bishops, or even a general council—fall into error and heresy; but only one solitary individual including a woman, or even baptized children, could remain untainted to preserve Christ's faith to the end, as he promised. For that reason, restoration of the church and its regulation according to faith are open to all believers, including laymen from the emperor downwards; indeed only if all agree, or at least none dissents, can a new article of faith be promulgated. Ockham's political writings abound with all the different contingencies in which the emperor can intervene to depose a pope, and the pope an emperor, and the faithful depose or elect one or other. The total effect is to dissolve any fixed institutional or sacramental boundaries between spiritual and temporal and to make each and every believer subject to the same law of Christ either directly contained in the Bible or in conformity with it. Only when all assent to it can it be regarded as the true faith and therefore of the universal church.

Ockham thus goes further than anyone along the road to individual judgment, based upon faith, at the expense of the hierarchy. While not, unlike Marsilius or Wycliffe, denying the latter any of its traditional attributes, Ockham effectively undermined its indispensability by reposing all canonical authority in the authority of the universal church mediated by scripture and reason. Faith was the only regulator; and observance of it the condition of membership of the church and authority within it. It could therefore be exercised by any of the faithful in default of its proper exercise by those ordained to do so. At the same time there was nothing of the biblical fundamentalist about Ockham. Just because of the contingency of all creation there is no immutably fixed order within the church or outside it. Neither pope nor emperor nor any other office was necessary of its own nature; nor need it be regulated in a fixed way. Christ did not decree how his successors should be elected. That is why there is no mention of the pope in the Bible. But equally to hold an office once created does not suffice to enjoy an authority which is not properly fulfilled. Hence in cases of necessity or utility the ordinary processes can be superseded, and a pope or an emperor be deposed in diverse ways, to which Ockham devotes pages in enumerating. It was there in his institutional flexibility that he was to be influential upon a conciliarist like Peter d'Ailly.

What all these thinkers, and, in an indirect way, the popular movements that echo many of their emphases, have in common is a reinterpretation of the source and the nature of spiritual power away from its institutional forms to conformity with Christ's life and teachings. In almost every case it meant the exclusion of the hierarchy from the dialogue between the individual believer and Christ, with his word, not the sacramental power of the church, as mediator. It made for a new stress upon spirituality which, whether it took an apocalyptic or a directly antisacerdotal form, was impelled by the same ideal of a return to an archetypal church. As such, together with the pursuit of God directly through individual experience, it gave a new orientation to the spiritual life of the fourteenth and fifteenth centuries.

Conclusion

If this book has shown anything it is the pluralism in the outlook of the fourteenth century. Within a common binding framework of absolute presuppositions, virtually every facet of knowledge and belief underwent reinterpretation, or rather a series of separate interpretations. For it was the renunciation of previous attempts to unite all knowledge and belief within a single system which marks the beginning of the dissolution of the medieval world outlook. That diversity extended beyond those areas considered in this book to the spread of humanistic interests, to be seen in the new classicizing activities of friars like Robert Holcot, Thomas Waleys, and John Ridevall, who adorned their sermons with illustrations drawn from antiquity, as well as in book collecting, and the parallel growth of vernacular literature, in which it may be recalled Eckhart and the Rhineland and English mystics wrote and preached. All these represented, if not self-contained, at least distinct sectors that were pursued for themselves to an extent which had not previously occurred, as we have considered in philosophy, theology, the study of nature, and spiritual life. That very dissolution, therefore, of the attempt to integrate them had as its accompaniment a new diversification and for a time a new fertility. But it could only go so far without overturning the very presuppositions upon which it proceeded. Hence its limitations. Which is what this book has also attempted to indicate.

None of the developments with which we have concerned here went beyond a certain point, and most of them had lost their impetus by the beginning of the fifteenth century. Only Wycliffe and Cusa of later medieval thinkers attempted the kind of reinterpretation that had occurred in the earlier and middle decades of the fourteenth century. Both failed because they still remained bound by those absolute presuppositions to which they could offer no feasible alternative: Wycliffe sought to put the philosophical clock back to an extreme realism which had long lost any credibility; Cusa both tried too much, in rejecting the very basis of Aristotelian logic on which any discourse was founded, and achieved too little in substituting a mathematical neoplatonizing mysticism that was inadequate for natural reason or knowledge of the world. Each in different ways exemplifies the failure of later medieval thinkers, of wishing to break out of the impasse without the will or the means to break with the modes—in the case of Wycliffe—or the absolute presuppositions—in the case of both of them—which held them within the existing outlook. Not that they should be necessarily criticized for that. The kind of intellectual certainty desired by Wycliffe and intellectual liberation demanded by Cusa were not to be had by merely redefining the terms of discourse. The very assumptions on which it was founded need redefinition. Not surprisingly that was a task too great for any individual intellect and too daunting for any believer; it demanded the combined effort of a religious Reformation and a scientific revolution extending over a century to bring it about. For it was precisely in those areas where practice and experience increasingly conflicted with precept and presupposition that the transformation from a medieval to a nonmedieval outlook occurred. That it took so long to come was just because of the hold that those precepts and presuppositions exercised. Rather than face the challenge of renouncing them, the thinkers of the later fourteenth and fifteenth centuries for the most part contented themselves with repeating the revisions to them made by their predecessors earlier in the fourteenth century. Only in religious life, where the spiritual tensions were increasingly hard to contain within the existing structure of the church, did the momentum increase. Elsewhere there was a notable loss of intellectual nerve where mere repetition of what had gone before produced the intellectual barrenness which helped to engender the subsequent reaction against scholasticism. But that took two centuries to make itself felt in new modes of thought which, when they came with Descartes and Spinoza, left little of the intellectual landscape that Cusa had wished to preserve.

If there is a conclusion to be drawn from this book it is perhaps that great and fundamental changes of outlook do not come in an instant. The dissolution of the medieval outlook was the work of centuries. But it was nonetheless revolutionary and far-reaching. There is a time-lag that enables men to continue to live with discontinuities long after they have occurred. It is due to the principle of inertia which is as strong in human society as in nature; but in society it has the added element of will, in wanting to continue in the same attitudes, often long after they have become intellectually untenable or practically inconsistent. Only when they become so irreconcilable that they contradict the very ends they are supposed to serve are they usually abandoned, and then not without a struggle, and a rearguard action extending in some cases over centuries, as in the persistence of a geocentric theory of the universe or in the Counter-Reformation. The dissolution of which we have been speaking, then, was not some sudden cataclysmic event; nor was it merely a negative rejection of all existing presuppositions; but their gradual supersession by new ones in a process of erosion that began in the fourteenth century and was only completed three centuries later when their full implications were finally recognized.

Index